HOW TO BUY A

FRANCHISE

EMPLOYEE TO
ENTREPRENEUR
IN 12 WEEKS

BY PATRICK **FINDARO**

ISBN: 9798870519289

Imprint: Independently published

TABLE OF CONTENTS

"Keep your feet on the ground and your eyes toward the stars."

Theodore Roosevelt

Are you ready to be your own boss?

Are you craving the flexibility that comes with owning a profitable business?

Franchising provides an opportunity for you to be in business for yourself but not by yourself. Provided the right business opportunity, franchising can be a win-win for the franchisor and franchisee.

As with kitesurfing, my preferred sport here in Miami Beach, it is safer and generally more enjoyable when you have a partner or even a community of riders. Kitesurfing involves launching and landing a powerful kite capable of propelling you 50 feet in the air! Only select advanced riders with years of experience are comfortable launching, riding, and landing unassisted. The vast majority of riders are happy to have a community of kiters to support in critical moments of the sport and trade notes on best practices.

That being said, you do not want someone brand new to kiting to launch your kite or trust you to give you the lowdown on a certain kite spot. There could be rocks submerged right off the coast, or wind fluctuations depending on the time of day.

Franchising makes sense when the franchisor has a well-established, replicable business model that has passed the test of time. You also want a community of successful business owners who are going to share best practices and be listened to by the franchisor to improve the overall system performance. Your success as a franchise owner will be largely based on the franchisor's executive and management team together with the community of franchisees in the system. If you are striving to earn $200,000+ a year as a business owner, look to other franchisees and see if they are hitting your earning objectives without slaving away working 70+ hour weeks (unless you're fine with that!).

My brother and I founded our first company, Visa Franchise, in an apartment in Miami Beach back in 2015. At Visa Franchise (www.visafranchise.com), we have advised more than 500 investors and interviewed thousands of franchisees and franchisors.

In 2019, we made our offline database available to the world, creating the most accessible, extensive resource of franchising information available through our company Vetted Biz (www.vettedbiz.com). You might have come across our company's capabilities through our YouTube videos or our podcast episodes on Franchise Findings, where we share our franchise insights for free.

Based on our experience, we have developed a program for you to become a franchise owner in just 12 weeks! With our accelerated program, you will have the ability to filter through thousands of franchises on an expedited basis to find that one needle in a haystack! Because of our expertise along with hundreds of interviews with franchisors and franchisees, you will have tools at your disposal to sift through information on many industries and different business models.

Instead of potentially taking one year to identify the best franchise opportunities for your future business selection, you will only need to spend 12 weeks by following the steps, studying the data, and learning from the case studies in our guide.

Since the 1990s, more than 8,000 franchise-based businesses in the U.S. have sought franchisees to expand their operations. However, fewer than 1,000 of these franchise models have had sustained success for more than a decade.

Because most franchise agreements have a term of 10 years, it is essential that you, as an investor, choose a franchise that makes financial sense and matches your career and lifestyle aspirations. The key to your success is choosing the right franchise "fit." Investigate different types of business alliances and conduct your due diligence before settling on your long-term business partner.

Each week, this guide provides vital information and steps to find the best franchise to own. The first three weeks are focused on helping you get your "house in order" before diving into your research and due diligence on franchises.

Weeks 4 to 9 involve extensive research into franchise brands and the franchisees who are operating in those franchise systems. We simplify it so you can save time and potentially significant money by not investing in the wrong franchise system or location.

In week 10 you will solidify your finances for investing in the business, then in week 11 you will negotiate the final terms with the franchisor before signing the agreement in week 12. After you are done with this sprint training, you'll be comfortable to continue running the marathon that is business ownership.

If by going through this exercise you decide a franchise is not for you, you will have all the facts to continue working at a company. As an alternative, you would have learned an incredible amount about small businesses and different industries to potentially start your own business or explore buying an existing business for sale. These alternative paths generally take more time and we recommend you start the entrepreneurial journey by exploring franchising with us over 12 weeks. At that point, you can decide the right avenue for you!

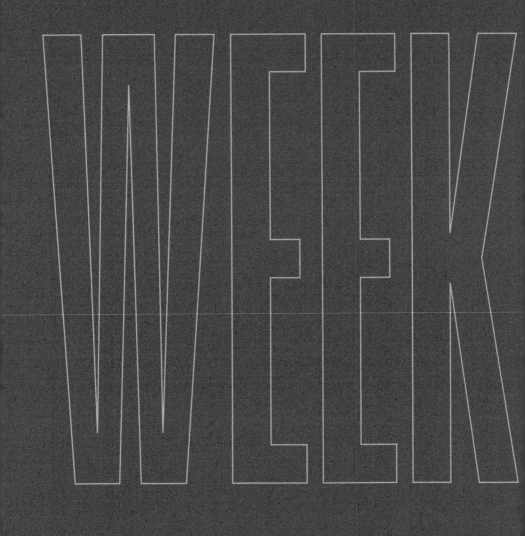

1

WHAT ARE YOUR GOALS AND OBJECTIVES IN LIFE?

"If you work just for money, you'll never make it, but if you love what you're doing and you always put the customer first, success will be yours."

Ray Kroc

Many people spend their whole lives dedicated to finding their purpose in life.

It is essential to be introspective in identifying your goals and objectives before you start investigating franchises or other business opportunities.

Franchising is a proven way to start a business because it allows you to basically sell an established product or service without having to start from "ground zero." A highly profitable business enterprise is possible through a franchise if you execute the model correctly with the right franchise system.

The following are some key issues you should focus on as you start your franchising journey:

COMPENSATION EXPECTATIONS:

Compensation in the franchising industry can vary greatly. Some of the top franchises like Wendy's experience franchise owner compensation in the range of $300,000 annually per location. If you do more business than the average franchise owner then your earnings can be significantly higher. Some franchise owners make as little as $20,000 annually but only allocate a few hours per week to the business. For example, with over 800 U.S. locations as of 2022, Sign Gypsies is the largest and fastest-growing yard sign greeting company. Sign Gypsies yard greeting rentals cater to homes, schools, and businesses. Most franchisees run their Sign Gypsies business as a side hustle to bring in additional income for their family.

REACHING COMPENSATION GOALS DOES NOT HAPPEN OVERNIGHT:

When starting off, your compensation might be relatively low or nonexistent. However, as you establish a larger customer base and gain their loyalty, you should start earning more. We estimate that it can take one to three years for a franchise to start making close to its potential earnings. This, however, varies depending on the industry and the location. Therefore, when looking at a franchise, you should conduct your due diligence into the financial viability of the franchise (reviewed in week 6 of this guide). At Vetted Biz, we provide payback period estimates, but this is just a start in the process of verifying key financial figures in greater depth with franchisees.

YOUR TIME COMMITMENT CAN VARY:

Depending on what your business is, and how much money you want to make, you could be working the same amount of hours you would work in a full-time job. Alternatively, you could basically maintain absentee ownership with less than five hours a week. Your time commitment will depend on which franchise you have opened and whether you want to pay for additional staff members.

When you are starting your business, you might be working many hours without taking any money home. This is typical when starting any business, including a franchise business. Years later, you might have the option to transition to absentee ownership where the business runs itself with controls in place and you are able to maintain a reliable income stream with significantly less time and effort. We all strive to "work smarter, not harder".

CASE STUDY:

BRUCE TURKEL

Passion, Purpose, And Pay

Building a successful franchise from scratch and increasing your return on investment along the way.

Back in 1966, the Turkel family opened a fruit stand in Miami that eventually became the Orange Bowl. The Orange Bowl was a snack bar with hot dogs, pizza, soft-serve ice cream, and sodas. Over the years,

Bruce Turkel spent his time working with franchisees so they could take advantage of what the franchisor (his family) provided. Bruce developed an expertise in branding and marketing and has always advised franchisors and franchisees to look for opportunities to enhance their business.

Bruce believes you can obtain your investment back and then build upon the brand through a multi-step process. At the outset, the franchisee pays for the operation and invests in it, putting his money where his mouth is, or as one might say "having skin in the game." The successful businessman steps into a system that works and uses it to increase value and income.

A franchise founder like Colonel Harlan Sanders opened one Kentucky Fried Chicken (KFC) store and wanted to make sure he understood the fundamentals and addressed mistakes from the first store before a second one was launched. (It is worth noting that at age 65 Sanders began franchising his chicken business using his $105 monthly social security check.) Today, KFC operates more than 5,200 restaurants in the U.S. and more than 15,000 units around the world.

Bruce also believes that overhead should be managed in a way that avoids excess charges unnecessary to operate the business. The customer does not care about multiple operations with fancy designs –**they are seeking a product or a service that meets their needs at the present time.** The business owner must always maintain his sense of focus so that his attention is not diverted away from the objective of maximizing his investment.

Too many locations for a franchise could also "chip away at what you worked so hard to build". And finally, Bruce advises that you "work on your business, not in your business". In other words, run the business by having the right people "behind the counter serving pizzas" or "installing the gutters".

As an entrepreneur, it is vital to "**balance passion, purpose & pay**". Bruce coined that phrase, and we will dive further into its application for business owners.

BALANCE PASSION, PURPOSE, AND PAY:

There are tremendous opportunities in the franchising industry with over 750,000 franchise locations in operation in the U.S. as of 2022. You will need to find what best suits your goals by balancing passion, purpose, and pay. For example, if you are more passionate about social work and contributing to society, you might want to look into franchises in education and senior care that will equip you to offer such special services to your community.

ARE COMPLICATED OR SIMPLE BUSINESS MODELS BEST?:

After studying 8,000+ franchises, we have found that the most profitable businesses are so complex that many potential investors are hesitant to take up the challenge. Many people want a simple retail business like 7-Eleven or something they can be passionate about like fitness or healthy food. Because of significant competition in these arenas, the margins generally are reduced for those offering such goods or services.

The franchising business model has penetrated a wide variety of industries in the United States. Popular chains like McDonald's, Domino's, and Pizza Hut are iconic restaurant brands, but there are many other franchise brands well known in their select industry.

If you like the home services sector or the janitorial sector, there are franchises like JAN-PRO (over 8,000 cleaning franchisees) with outstanding customer recognition and operational processes. There are so many industries to choose from that it can quickly become difficult to figure out where to start. If you need more help in identifying what industry might be a good fit for you, then take our Entrepreneur Quiz (www.vettedbiz.com/quiz-test).

IT IS IMPORTANT TO WEIGH THE PROS AND CONS OF OWNING A FRANCHISE:

We are not providing our opinion in this book on each individual situation. While different types of businesses and work models can be utilized for different kinds of people, franchising presents a viable option to start a business. If you have the right franchise, you can ultimately earn a significant amount of money. Likewise, the wrong franchise in the wrong location can lose an investor a lot of money and lead to bankruptcy.

We advise you to consider carefully the pros and cons of buying and running a franchise before making your selection.

CHECKLIST

☐ Identify and define your values. They will guide your decisions.

☐ Focus on your priorities.

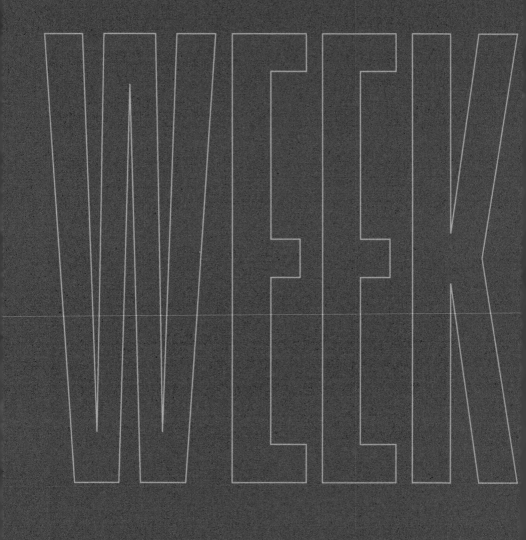

2.

FINANCING YOUR FRANCHISE: EQUITY (CASH), DEBT, AND ALTERNATIVES

"Cash is king."

Pehr G. Gyllenhammar

Starting a business is challenging – you need business acumen, industry knowledge, and a solid work ethic. However, the most important ingredient is money. Remember the maxim "Money does not talk – it screams"? You need money for a host of activities such as paying invoices, building out your location, advertising your business, and hiring employees and consultants.

A franchise can provide you with a proven business model to use, and if executed correctly it should lead to high compensation. However, starting and running a franchise often requires a large sum of capital at the outset ($100,000+). You need significant startup capital to pay for legal services, acquire the real estate, buy the initial inventory, and the list goes on.

If you do not have the finances to start the franchise on your own, you can consider bringing on partners who can help finance the project. This investor can be a friend, family member, or even a work colleague. You might get lucky and make it big on Shark Tank, but we would hedge our bets against that happening! With that said, if you choose the investor route, be aware that you will be giving up partial control of the business.

It is critical that you work with a partner who you trust entirely and whose goals align with yours. It is in your best interest to draw up a solid partnership operations agreement that outlines everyone's responsibilities, rights, and allocation of profits.

SAVINGS

This is the easiest way to start a franchise. You tap into the money you have already saved and invest it in your business. However, this also should come with the risk that if the business does not succeed, you could lose your "nest egg."

FRIENDS AND FAMILY

If you do not have enough money for the franchise you want to start, you might want to consider obtaining funds from family and friends, who could act as lenders or investors. Your focus should be on longtime, trustworthy friends who know you well and with whom you have shared business ideas in a variety of settings before approaching them to invest.

A familiar example is asking friends and family to donate to a charity race you are running. You can ask once or twice but it is difficult to do so on a regular basis over a number of years. With respect to a franchise investment, if friends and family are not interested in investing initially, they could feel pressured to invest due to the relationship. However, everyone has to be cognizant that the relationship could be impaired if the business does not succeed.

HOME EQUITY LINE OF CREDIT (HELOC)

HELOC stands for "Home Equity Line of Credit." If you own a home, a bank can provide you a line of credit that is a home-based line of credit or a home equity loan. These options measure or estimate the value of the equity in your home to approve the loan or credit. Home equity is the difference between what your property is worth and what you owe on the property. For example, if a home is valued at $600,000, but you only have $200,000 left to pay on your mortgage, you have $400,000 in equity. However, most banks will not let you take out a loan for the entire equity amount. A home line of credit allows you to essentially access cash that is backed by the equity of your home. This can work particularly well when interest rates are low.

A downside of home equity loans is that you put your property at risk of forfeiture if you end up defaulting on your loan. Additionally, home equity loans require a high credit score and a solid debt-to-income ratio for approval.

401(K) ROLLOVERS FOR BUSINESS STARTUPS (ROBS)

Rollovers for Business Startups (ROBS) allow you to use your own retirement money to start your business, skipping the process of going to a lender entirely. To qualify for a ROBS plan, you need to have a 401(k), a 403(b), or an IRA account. These are all retirement savings plans often set up by your current or past employer.

You will also need to work with a ROBS provider to access the money. Retirement rollover providers generally charge a small, one-time fee as well as monthly maintenance fees for compliance purposes.

Normally, taking money out of your retirement fund has a host of associated fees and penalties. On the contrary, with ROBS, you can avoid these fees and access your money in just a matter of weeks. If you decide to leverage your retirement savings for your franchise investment, it is strongly recommended that you seek guidance from an advisor with a strong track record. Also, make sure your that CPA is comfortable with the structure because not all structures are compliant with the IRS rules.

If you invest a significant amount of your retirement money in a franchise, you may no longer have a solid diversification of bonds and/or stocks for your retirement. Generally, the more concentrated the investment portfolio, the more unique risk the portfolio will have. Your retirement money will be in the hands of your business performance, for better or worse.

DEBT

SMALL BUSINESS ADMINISTRATION (SBA) LOAN

SBA loans are a popular choice for startup franchisees. The SBA is a government institution that facilitates long-term loans at competitive rates. The SBA does not actually provide loans but instead guarantees 75% to 85% of the loan from a bank or credit union. This is an excellent option for someone starting a franchise business or buying an existing franchise business.

There are two types of SBA loans: the SBA 7A and the SBA CDA/504 loans.

SBA 7A loans offer individuals up to **$5 million** with repayment terms ranging from 7-25 years. These loans can be used for multiple purposes depending on the terms and conditions of your loan including real estate or franchise fees. Similar to most loans, the interest rates for these loans will depend on the amount and length of the loan (generally prime + 2.75%).

The SBA CDA/504 loan involves a collaborative effort, typically broken down into:

• A nonprofit Certified Development Company (CDA) provides up to

40% of the amount needed by the franchisee.

- A bank or credit union provides up to **50%** of the amount.

- The franchisee contributes the remainder of around **10%**.

With an SBA CDA/504 loan, there are limitations on how the funding can be used. For example, you cannot use the loan to pay franchise fees.

While a SBA loan is easier to acquire than a business loan from traditional lenders, it is still a time-consuming process and requires the borrower to have an acceptable credit score.

FRANCHISE PARTNERSHIPS

In a partnership, the level of investment can be as low as **$10,000**. That is the case for popular brands Chick-fil-A and Steak 'n Shake, which we will review further. Essentially, the company builds the whole store for you and provides you with inventory and everything else essential for business operations. You would be in partnership with the company for the store's management. This partnership can vary from you just being an employee of the company to you being a contractual partner. In due time, you might also be able to buy the location from the franchisor and become a full owner, but that depends on the franchisor and your contractual arrangements with the company.

Chick-fil-A partnership. For the uninitiated, the Chick-fil-A franchise serves fried chicken in a quick-service restaurant model. Chick-fil-A opened its first stand-alone location in Atlanta, Georgia in 1986. Back then they started store traditions such as their famous "Sunday closures," which remain a part of their business model to this day. Today, Chick-fil-A currently has more than 2,300 stores in the United States that generate on average $6 million in sales (2022). Chick-fil-A's headquarters is still located in Atlanta and owned by the Cathy family.

The company's franchise model deviates from most others. Chick-fil-A is financially responsible for all startup costs including real estate, restaurant construction, and store equipment. Moreover, Its franchisee rents the location for an initial investment of **$10,000**; an ongoing royalty fee of **15%** and an additional fee of **50%** of pretax profit remain.

Despite the relatively simple initial financial requirements to own a Chick-fil-A franchise, the franchisor acceptance rate is as low as **0.4%**. Also, candidates have to undergo an extensive application profile. This includes being one of the 80 applicants selected among the more than 20,000 inquiries. With this much interest to become a Chick-fil-A franchise, clearly they are doing something right!

Among the top fast-food franchises, Chick-fil-A was ranked #1 in sales per restaurant at $6.1 million annually. This number is surprising given that all of its stores are closed on Sundays. Also, it only operates 2,225 restaurants – less than one-sixth as many as the top three earning franchise-type restaurants ranked by QSR magazine.

Operators can expect to earn 50% of the restaurant profits while the Cathy family earns the other 50% and maintains ultimate ownership of the 2,300+ restaurants. Operators regularly earn $200,000 to $400,000 managing one or two Chick-fil-A restaurants.

This structure has allowed the Cathy family to amass a fortune of ~$14 billion (2022). It's not bad to be closely associated with a billionaire family!

Steak 'n Shake also offers a similar opportunity. The Steak 'n Shake franchise is a classic American brand serving premium burgers and milkshakes.

For a total investment of **$10,000**, selected franchisees (who are called Franchise Partners) are granted the rights necessary to operate a franchised Steak 'n Shake restaurant. Once you become a Franchise Partner of **Steak 'n Shake** with a **$10,000** investment, you earn **50%** of the restaurant's profits.

SETTING UP YOUR LOAN OPTION FOR A RAINY DAY

Even if you want to invest mostly cash, it would be advisable to seek a line of credit from a bank. It is much easier to get approved for a loan pre-launch or with a profitable business than it would be once you have a business that is "bleeding" money. Multiple franchisees who have appeared on our *Franchise Findings* podcast, including Mosquito Hunters and Molly Maids, have emphasized the loan option as a backup if needed. It can be difficult to predict macroeconomic trends, and what a difference an extra 3-6+ months of cash can make to keeping your business open or deciding to close it permanently.

First-time entrepreneurs should be cautious with the amount of debt they take on and must be prepared for the worst-case scenario. Not only could you lose your capital investment but also your home as collateral. Also, there could be obligations due to the landlord for unpaid rents as well as unpaid royalties to the franchisor if you close the business early. It is important to work with a business finance specialist to help navigate the loan approval process (or retirement rollover).

A skilled attorney can negotiate the franchise agreement with the franchisor and lease agreement with the landlord to minimize your potential liability.

CASE STUDY: JOSH AMBROSE

And Mosquito Hunters

How to start a franchise and set up a financing plan

Franchise Started in January 2021

Previous Experience: Military and Banking

Franchise: Mosquito Hunters

Josh Ambrose is a franchisee of Mosquito Hunters in Jacksonville as well as St. Augustine, Florida. Mosquito Hunters use licensed and trained technicians to target and kill mosquitoes, ticks, and fleas immediately and create a barrier that keeps them from coming back.

When Josh looked at setting up a business with a franchise broker, for a specific territory, he saw a low startup cost with real profit potential. Josh decided to purchase a Mosquito Hunters franchise because he had the drive to be his own boss and to own a business.

At the start of the franchise journey, Josh believes that the business owner has to set up a financing plan. At the outset, Josh identified three sources of income (including his wife's) and tax refunds to help fund the business and utilized accounting expertise. Much of his early costs related to marketing. Josh focused on a franchise for which the startup costs were not high and that did not have building or leasing costs; he planned to start it as a home-based business. He also focused on a business with recurring revenues; he thinks that a franchise owner should have operations in at least two territories.

Josh believes a franchisee should work with a company that has a solid "ground game" and is willing to assist in marketing through social media and other venues (like door hangers and road signs). Communication with other Mosquito Hunters franchisees as well as customer service also helps in enhancing the business.

Empowering his team has been a key to Josh's success. He believes in delegating tasks, sharing experiences, maintaining a positive mindset, and not micromanaging employees. Currently, Josh has 220 clients, both residential and commercial. Having the flexibility to adjust to seasonal markets and knowing how to operate within the customer's family unit to get them to enroll in their seasonal programs are also important.

As a former Marine Corps officer, Josh always improves his "fighting hole." A positive, growth-minded approach where the business owner is always learning and trying to improve can bring much success. Time efficiency, seizing opportunities, and facing challenges are also critical.

Words of wisdom from Josh:

1. Don't close the doors on any opportunity.

2. Listen to what people have to say.

3. Know yourself. If you have a drive, you'll do well. If you don't have a drive, maybe being in business ownership is not for you.

4. And then lastly, think about how to fund your business." He recommends that funding should come from an SBA loan on the front end with self-funding on the back end, in case you do not grow as fast as projected or in case unplanned expenses occur. **Ongoing financing should always be part of business planning.** How to fund your startup business should be at the top of the list.

CHECKLIST

☐ Ensure you have significant startup capital ($100,000+).

☐ Consider business partners with whom you trust entirely and whose goals align with yours.

3

YOUR TRUSTED ADVISORS: SUPPORT WITH FINDING, VETTING, AND INVESTING IN A FRANCHISE

"If you want to run fast, run alone. If you want to run far, run together."

African proverb

"If everyone is moving forward together, then success takes care of itself."

Henry Ford

When starting a franchise, you will need certain experts by your side to navigate the system and help you address all the responsibilities associated with a franchise. Some of these people must be hired, and are non-negotiable for success, while other types are strongly advised. Let's look at non-negotiable advisors first.

A FRANCHISE ATTORNEY IS CRITICAL

If you run a business on any scale, legal counsel will be required. While theoretically you can do much on your own (in at least some states), it is best practice to hire a franchise attorney. Franchise attorneys have been trained in this specialty of the law and can lighten your load. In some states, a business or a business owner cannot represent themselves and an attorney or lawyer is necessary by law if litigation arises.

With an attorney, you can hedge your bets against legal problems in the future. A good lawyer is going to be a valuable resource in addressing any legal questions and in providing legal services that you might require. Whether it is negotiating the franchise agreement, handling employment issues, or litigation, an experienced business attorney should be by your side.

One of the best ways to source potential business attorneys is through your own personal or professional network. Recommendations should be solicited from a trusted friend or family member, or from a business colleague in the same industry, particularly where your interests are aligned. You might also consider asking for a recommendation from someone you already work with – like your bookkeeper or accountant. Make sure the attorney does have experience with franchising as it is a specific subset of business law.

Local organizations helping small businesses, or organizations like the Small Business Association (SBA), can also help you find a lawyer. Also, the Association of Franchisees and Dealers (AAFD) offers a network of franchise attorneys to support new and existing franchisees.

That said, it is important to perform your due diligence to vet any lawyer you find. Be sure to check their online reviews, bar status, and types of clients they represent.

REAL ESTATE ATTORNEY (FOR LONG-TERM LEASES/PURCHASING PROPERTY)

A real estate attorney can help you negotiate your lease for wherever you want to start a business. There is a lot of fine print that goes into leasing (or even buying) a place for you to do business, and an attorney can help you make sure everything is in order. You might even be buying the whole building or constructing a franchise like a preschool from the ground up. In all those cases a real estate attorney is vital!

However, for flexible or short-term leases like a WeWork or Regus workspace, you might not need a real estate attorney.

Now, let's look at some types of advisors who are highly recommended to retain:

RECOMMENDED ADVISORS

Franchise Broker, Coach, or Consultant

A broker, by definition, connects a buyer and a seller. In the eyes of a person new to doing business, a consultant might be someone who will provide advice on businesses. There are three different categories when it comes to these relationships.

Franchise brokers are generally only compensated if a candidate whom they represent moves forward and invests in a franchise with that franchisor who's paying the commission. Franchise brokers receive varying degrees of training dependent on the network(s) they are associated with. Most brokers have strong sales acumen, and the best brokers have prior experience in franchising (as franchisors and/ or franchisees). A franchise broker might call themselves a franchise consultant, franchise advisor, or franchise coach.

The job of a **franchise consultant** is to offer expert advice to prospective franchisees to help them determine if they are suitable for franchise ownership and, if so, which franchise or industry might suit them best to align with their goals. The consultant's job is to educate the prospective franchisee about the industry and work with them to find the best franchise opportunities based on their interests, budget, and skills. There are select franchise coaches who receive an hourly or flat fee and who might not be compensated by the franchisor. Be sure to understand clearly how the franchise broker/coach is compensated and if there is an agreement or code of conduct.

When my brother and I founded Visa Franchise in 2015, we decided to focus on a specific niche: foreign nationals buying franchises in the U.S. This group of franchise buyers represents less than 5% of the market but is often willing to pay for an advisor (Visa Franchise) to find and analyze the franchises AND to secure smooth passage to the U.S. for them and their families. We often charge an upfront engagement fee in excess of $10,000, allowing us to support clients investigating franchises independent of whether the franchise provides a finder fee. We even helped a client secure the franchise license to open 20+ International House of Pancakes (IHOP) and received NO compensation from IHOP for referring our client to their franchise brand.

If you have purchased a home with support of a buyer's agent, then you are likely a good fit for using a franchise broker. In other words, did you have a realtor support you with finding your dream home or did you contact the seller directly through a website like Zillow.com? If you prefer to interact directly with the seller and not have buyer representation, then you can opt to contact the franchisor directly. Each path has its pros and cons. Unlike a home, though, a business is largely an intangible asset where the financial recovery is very low until it produces $5,000+ of income per month. In other words, if you have buyer's regret, you cannot simply sell the business like you could a home for a 5-10% cut.

In case you choose not to work with a franchise consultant/broker, expect the process to take longer and plan to lean harder on your other advisors like the franchise attorney.

Accountant

Questions to consider: Are you forming a corporation or an LLC? What is the best corporate structure? How will taxes be handled? An accountant would certainly help address these issues (in conjunction with a business lawyer).

LLC stands for limited liability company. LLCs can be set up through individual states. LLCs have few requirements and are attractive because of their liability protection and potential tax savings. This means that any debts and liabilities incurred to the business are separated from the business owners. Many first-time entrepreneurs think there is a fiscal benefit to opening an LLC domiciled in Delaware. However, these benefits are generally reserved for large corporations; 99% of franchisees who choose the LLC route open in the state of operations.

S Corporations are for smaller companies, because they are only allowed to have up to 100 owners. Furthermore, owners are only able to receive common stock, meaning that there are no preferred voting shares. S Corporations are only taxed once but do have ongoing compliance fees. S Corporations also require all owners to be U.S. citizens or residents.

Whether you set up your company as an S Corp, LLC, or any other business structure, you will need an accountant to maintain and keep your books. Your company will also have ongoing yearly documents like financial statements and tax returns that an accountant can best handle.

Support with Financing

For those who are homeowners, you probably either worked directly with a bank or through a mortgage broker for your home's financing. If you worked with a mortgage broker, he probably "shopped" your application around for the best deal/structure with various lenders.

For SBA loans, the financing rate and structure is pretty similar bank to bank, as opposed to mortgage banks whose rates can vary a full 1%! For loans above $50,000, the rate is capped at Prime + 2.75%; few banks offer a rate below this.

Financing Consultant (Loan Broker)

Financing consultants will analyze your personal financials together with those of the franchise. The specialist will explain all the SBA loan programs and financing options available to then prepare a loan package to submit to SBA lenders. Some consultants can also support you with the 401(k) rollover even in tandem with the SBA loan.

After that, the consultant will find the right SBA lender to fund the chosen franchise business. The financing specialist then works with you to prepare all the documents and paperwork needed for the bank's loan underwriting process. Top consultants are by your side from the beginning until the end (business funded).

SBA lenders often have concentrations in specific industries, as well as states/regions of the U.S. Leading consultants have relationships with many of the SBA lenders.

An experienced consultant can speed up the overall funding process by weeks or even months. They can do this by "hedging bets" between different banks and applying to a few different banks for funding. That way, he sets up a plan B or C in case the top bank rejects your loan application weeks into the process.

Consultants generally charge an upfront fee of $2,500 to $5,000 and might charge an additional fee of 1-3% of the total loan amount at funding.

The upfront fee covers their costs/time to complete your applications, package all documents, and then shop your application across SBA lenders.

Our company Vetted Biz has developed a funding solution to bypass the need for a financing consultant at no cost to the borrower. For more information on this solution visit our site at www.vettedbiz.com/funding-product/

Ask How Quickly on Average They Can Secure the SBA Loan

From the time you provide them with the required documents and pay their fee, what is the average time it takes to receive funding? If they cannot answer this right away or after a day of asking for this data internally, that is a "red flag."

Consultants should not disclose your information without your consent. Therefore, you should ask how your information is stored and ask for assurance that your information is ONLY shared with prospective lenders and no one else.

Working Directly with the Bank (Bank Lender)

If you prefer to work directly with a lender, you need to find one who is comfortable with the industry and franchise brand you are most interested in. Just because you have a business banking relationship does not mean they will finance you for a different franchise business.

Further along in the process, you can ask the franchisors/franchisees for direct referrals of banks that have already funded loans to franchisees of the system in the past. If the bank does not have experience already with the franchise brand you are investing in, the process will most likely take more time than with a consultant who "hedges your bets" with multiple financial institutions.

CHECKLIST

☐ Perform your due diligence when vetting advisors.

☐ Ask for client references and/or testimonials.

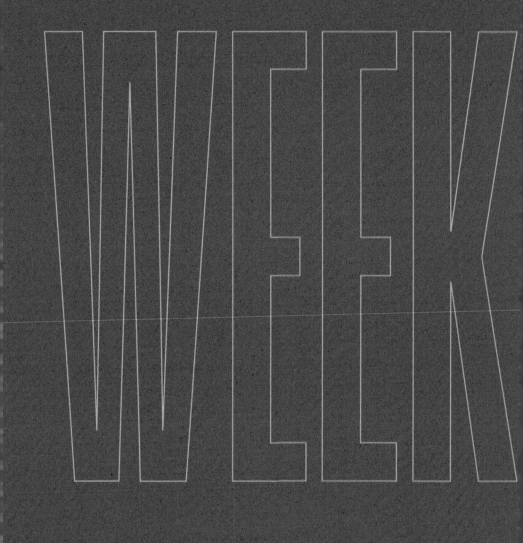

4 INITIAL FRANCHISE SEARCH

"You can't plan for everything, or you never get started in the first place."

Jim Butcher, Changes

"As long as one keeps searching, the answers come."

Joan Baez

For your search, you should look at several different options. While exploring your franchise choice, these are the main factors you should consider:

Investment Amount: The most important consideration is the investment amount. The investment range to open a franchise − including the franchise fee, working capital, and any real estate expenses − are included in Item 7 of the Franchise Disclosure Document (FDD).

Revenues (Sales): Another important item is the revenue projection. How much money will you be making from this franchise before expenses? (Sales and revenue outside of the U.S. is often called turnover.) Sixty percent of franchises disclose financial information, generally at least the sales information in Item 19 of the FDD. If the franchisor does not disclose sales information, it is essential that you consult directly with multiple franchisees. Revenues are often noted as average unit volume (AUV). AUV and/or total systemwide sales are published for the largest franchise brands at qsrmagazine.com, Franchisetimes.com, and restaurantbusinessonline.com.

Net Income (Owner Benefit): A third important consideration is how much money does the franchise make in terms of net income, and owner's benefit? In other words, how much are you making from the business to benefit directly you and your family? Unfortunately, less than 25% of franchises provide this information in Item 19 of the franchise disclosure document. You will need to talk with franchisees to better understand how much they are making in Year 1, Year 2, and Year 3, and what the general trend is for income generation for that particular franchise.

Sales/Investment Ratio: In lieu of comparing the net income across franchise brands, data does exist on the average sales (sometimes estimated) and investment midpoint for thousands of franchises. This can be a good proxy for comparing different franchise brands. Generally, if the sales to investment ratio is less than 1, that is a "red flag."

Pizza Franchise	Midpoint Investment	Average Unit Volume (Sales)	Sales/ Investment Ratio
Domino's	$419,475	$1,304,012	3.1
Papa John's	$412,715	$997,000	2.4
Marco's Pizza	$437,626	$838,000	1.9
Blaze Pizza	$865,450	$959,400	1.1
Little Caesars	$1,037,100	$951,000	0.9
Pizza Hut Traditional	$1,215,250	$973,000	0.8

Health Care Franchise	Midpoint Investment	Average Unit Volume (Sales)	Sales/ Investment Ratio
Home Instead	$116,500	$2,229,000	19.1
Synergy HomeCare	$92,094	$1,519,000	16.4
BrighStar Care	$151,058	$2,172,000	14.3
Right at Home	$121,794	$1,261,000	10.3
Senior Helpers	$122,600	$1,230,000	10.0
Touching Hearts at Home	$62,250	$566,000	9.0
Visiting Angels	$142,305	$1,250,000	8.7
FirstLight HomeCare	$155,800	$1,083,000	6.9
Interim HealthCare	$429,125	$2,670,000	6.2
Assisting Hands Home Care	$123,675	-	-

Franchise Failure Rate: The fourth consideration is the franchise failure rate. You need to know how many franchises are closing down. How many franchises are not extending after the initial 10-year term? How many franchises broke their agreement with the franchisor? In what instances did the relationship not make sense?

Franchise for Sale Rate: The fifth important consideration is the franchise sales rate, basically the transfer rate, as well as the franchisor buying back locations from franchisees. This can indicate that people do not want to continue to grow with the franchise system and they prefer to move on to some other entrepreneurial venture.

Take Snap-on tools, for example; 405 franchisees sold/transferred their license to new franchisees from 2019 to 2021. In that same period, the franchisor reacquired 600 units from franchisees. At the start of 2019, there were 3,327 franchised units open representing a 30% franchise for sale rate.

Another example, Dickey's Barbeque Pit; 217 of 500 locations were transferred or reacquired by the franchisor from 2019 to 2021. Many of their franchisees allegedly sold their BBQ restaurant to new franchisees for significantly less than the cost to build the restaurant out.

Do you want to be part of a franchise system like Snap-on where every three years, 30% of the franchisees are no longer involved in the brand? Or even worse, 43% as was the case with Dickey's Barbeque Pit?

Franchise Success Ratio: Number six is the "franchise success ratio." Hundreds of thousands of Small Business Administration (SBA) loans have been issued to franchisees throughout the United States. As an illustration we looked at 10 loans that were paid in full, where the franchisee was able to pay back the loan totally to the bank whereas only one defaulted. This would be a 10-to-1 loan success ratio for that particular franchise.

Top 20 Franchises By Success Ratio

Franchise	SBA Loan Success Ratio	Franchise	SBA Loan Success Ratio
Orange Theory Fitness	180:0	Sport Clips	135:0
The UPS Store	170:0	Domino's Pizza	132:1
Ameriprise Financial	114:0	Best Western Inn	118:1
Comfort/Comfort Inn & Suites	106:0	European Wax Center	105:1
Planet Fitness	88:0	Chevron (Gas Station)	92:1
Christian Brothers Automotive	72:0	Super 8	88:1
Choice Hotels International Inn	61:0	Red Roof Inn	83:1
Culver's	51:0	Jersey Mike's	74:1
Wingstop Restaurants	51:0	Allstate Insurance	66:1
Quality Inn/ Quality Suites Hotel	137:1	Dunkin Donuts	63:1

Bottom 20 Franchises By Success Ratio

Franchise	SBA Loan Success Ratio	Franchise	SBA Loan Success Ratio
Experimax	10:35	Meineke	20:16
Dental Fix Rx	9:21	Tutor Doctor	11:8
Embroidme	6:11	Mr. Appliance	7:5
Maid-Rite Sandwich Shop	4:7	Patrice & Associates	7:5
Window Genie	6:10	Orange Leaf Frozen Yogurt	19:13
Glass Doctor	5:6	CPR-Cell Phone Repair	6:4
Extreme Pita	6:6	Togo's	6:4
Tom and Chee	5:5	Fantastic Sams	19:12
Signarama	17:15	Arcpoint	10:6
Flip Flop Shops	7:6	Baja Fresh Mexican Grill	10:6

Franchise Industry Risk Data: Risk data is important to consider. We have the data for most types of franchises. We also know how that industry has done as a whole. So looking at food and beverage, for example, for a franchise over the last 10 years, our analysts have calculated that for every nine restaurant franchises that pay a loan back in full, one defaulted. When you look at some other industries like healthcare, real estate, and education, the default rate is lower. So, it is essential to examine the specific industry figures. A key indicator for that is the success rate of those who have taken out a loan to open up a business or franchise in that industry.

Macro Industry data: Is the industry growing like the clothing resale market or decreasing like the frozen yogurt and dessert markets?

That does not mean the franchise won't have success like Crumbl Cookies, which operates in the desserts industry but has average sales of $1.6M per store!

It just makes it harder to position and you do not get to benefit from the "tide rising all boats." To better understand how an industry is performing, there is a wide range of resources depending on your budget. The most economical is Google news and Google search. Type in the INDUSTRY NAME + industry. You can get a general idea of how the industry is performing through reviewing 5-10 articles. INDUSTRY NAME + Decline. Industry NAME + Growth.

John LaRosa's Marketdata Enterprises, Inc. was founded in 1979 and provides industry studies. They have an Overview Summary report on many industries available for just $99. The full report, similar to those produced by large market research firms like IBISWorld, will cost you $1,000+.

John's free blog provides key insights like how "the autism treatment market was estimated to be valued at $4.1 billion as of 2021, growing by 11%."

Resale Value: We recommend that you ask the franchisor about recent resales of franchises that have left the system. One business example would be a senior home care business. It is possible that you could invest

$150,000 to start the business (including working capital), and then after five years, you could sell the business for $500,000+.

CASE STUDY:

CURT MAIER

Exiting your franchise business for a profit and helping franchise & business buyers

Franchise Opened in 2005 and Successfully Exited in 2011

Previous Experience: Military and Multinational Executive

Franchise: SarahCare

Curt Maier is a business/franchise broker at the IBA (International Business Associates), and he is the only dual licensed business/franchise broker in the state of Washington. Curt understands the benefits of starting a new franchise compared with an existing business or a franchise resale.

After exploring a number of different franchise concepts, Curt decided on the senior health care space with SarahCare. In the Lehigh Valley (Pennsylvania) where Curt lived, there was a market to help people who had cognitive or physical impairments. Moreover, Curt focused on what he enjoyed, primarily sales and marketing instead of operations.

SarahCare is an adult daycare franchise, so an investment in a brick-and-mortar facility had to be made. At the outset, Curt hired and trained staff and negotiated his lease. It took approximately three years before he started seeing real progress, and ultimately he became a "full time absentee owner" after hiring someone to manage day-to-day operations. To live far from his business, Curt had to have full confidence in his employees and had to assure quality control. This was in the "pre-Zoom" days and long telephone calls and site visits made it work. He only sold his business because of an unsolicited offer.

"The average small business/franchise actually changes hands every 8 years! Think about that...less than the average 10 year initial term in a franchise agreement. It is vital that you think with the end in mind!" said Curt.

After selling his business, Curt said, "What I really wanted to do in life was to help people like me." He realized there was a market to help others to either buy or sell a business or franchise. This allowed Curt to continue being involved in franchising, where he found success. He has been able to offer his clients the ability to either buy an existing franchise or to start a new one where they would decide on location and the business model. Not steering his clients in any one direction, he gives his clients options with the pros and cons of choosing a particular path.

ENOUGH OF THE KEY METRICS TO TRACK – LET'S START THE FRANCHISE SEARCH!

To start your search, I encourage you (albeit I'm biased) to have a look at our website, Vetted Biz (**www.vettedbiz.com**).

There are also websites like Franchimp and Franchise Grade that list most franchises available, not just those paying to be advertised on the website.

I am not a fan of franchise portals like Franchise Direct, BizBuySell, and Franchise Gator that list (or heavily prioritize) franchises because they are paid by the franchise seller. BizBuySell is a good resource for existing franchises for sale but not franchise opportunities where you must start from ground zero. These portals often include "business opportunities" within the franchise section of their website. Business opportunities are far less regulated than franchises and allowed to make earnings claimed but not substantiated in their offering documents.

Also, the "Franchise 500" list by the famous publication *Entrepreneur* and other lists should be taken with a grain of salt. Many poor-performing franchises have been on this list for multiple years running.

9Round Kickboxing, for example, is one of five franchises prominently displayed on Franchise Direct's home page. 9Round was ranked #169 on the 2021 "Franchise 500" list. However, they closed nearly 115 locations in 2020, representing 20% of the kickboxing gyms open at the start of 2020.

In 2022, 9Round ranked #171 for Top Global Franchises, #78 for Top Franchises for Veterans, and #88 for Top Franchises for Less Than $150,000. *Entrepreneur* has numerous lists beyond the Franchise 500 ranking that, at the end of the day, do not mean much. Critics might blame the pandemic for their failure, but even in 2019 they closed more locations than they opened.

Franchise 500 Ranking History

Compare where 9Round Fitness landed on this year's Franchise 500 Ranking versus previous years.

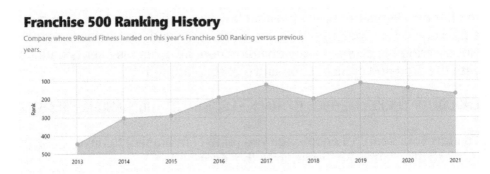

As of October 2022, 9Round is featured on the home page of Franchise Direct together with one of the worst franchise success ratio franchise brands, Tutor Doctor. From 2010 to 2020, for every 11 loans paid in full by Tutor Doctor franchisees, there have been eight charged off, unable to be paid back after default.

Franchises for Sale 2022, Starting at Under $10k!

Search the World's Largest Franchise Directory with 100s of Top Franchises

Industry   Investment   FIND THE BEST FRANCHISES ›

Browse Franchises by Category

LOW-COST FRANCHISES →   TOP FRANCHISES →   WORK FROM HOME →   HOT & TRENDING →

You should take a look at the businesses in your community if you want to narrow your industry focus. This will help you determine which ones you like and find interesting. You could potentially fill a business void in your community. With this approach, you would be providing a service that the community needs and you can earn income soon after opening because you would be the only provider in that geographic area. However, no competition in that business sector could be a warning sign that there is not a market for that franchise type.

What industries pique your interest? You can start by learning more about different franchises at www.vettedbiz.com/industries. Also, you could review the macro/industry information from third-party sources.

CHECKLIST

☐ Learn the language of the industry.

☐ Keep a log of your progress and keep track of key metrics.

5 CHECK FRANCHISE'S CRITERIA FOR OWNERSHIP & FIRST CALLS WITH FRANCHISORS

"There's a lid for every pot."

Yiddish proverb

"Matchmaker, matchmaker, make me a match, find me a find, catch me a catch."

Sheldon Harnick

Franchising is a two-way street that will never be complete without the franchisor and the franchisee coming together on the same terms. Many top-performing franchises like Domino's Pizza are exclusive on who is accepted into their system. For Domino's you already have to be employed as a manager before you can be considered as a franchisee (in the U.S.). In many cases you will find that with top franchises, you are required to already be working with the company for some time or at least in the industry.

To determine whether the franchise you are considering is right for you, it is critical to study the franchise's requirements. These are usually listed on the website in their franchising section. These can help you determine whether you have the prerequisites to start a franchise. The prerequisites usually include a minimum net worth with a specified portion in liquid assets. Also, some franchises will require experience in the industry.

The franchise or their website can also help you determine whether there is availability in your area. Some franchises only provide locations in certain geographic areas where they are looking to expand. If the franchise you want to start does not offer a location in your area, you might consider looking into existing locations of the franchise. Franchise development representatives might be compensated differently or not at all if it is a franchise resale. This should be asked of the franchise representatives. "Trust but verify" by checking on franchise resale websites like Franchise Flipper, Franchise Resales, and BizBuySell.

A franchise advisor can be helpful as you navigate the outreach and coordination of initial calls. Before talking to the franchisor, you should prepare a list of questions. These questions can help you determine whether the franchise is the right fit for you. Potential questions include: "What should I know about joining your franchise system? What does your introductory training program look like? What ongoing training do you offer once you are in the system?" Keep the first call "light" and avoid questions related to the legal terms of the franchise until the second call with the franchisor. Remember, it is a two-way process and the franchisor has their way of presenting the brand and taking you through the journey of discovery.

We recommend you speak with at least four franchisors, and at least two of them should be in different industries. These conversations can help you in your investigation and explore new industries you might have previously not considered.

HOW ABOUT FRANCHISE RESALES?

If there is a franchise available for resale in your desired area, this can be a tremendous opportunity to skip the startup phase. Be sure to ask the franchise development representative if there are any available resales and if he can assist you in connecting with the seller. You need to ask in the right way because the franchise adviser (representing you) and the franchise development representative (representing the franchisor) might not be compensated at the same rate or at all if you decide to move forward with the resale.

Depending on their modus operandi, they might connect you with the business broker representing the seller or with the seller directly. Some franchise developers and consultants might dismiss franchise resales and present varying reasons to avoid them. Keep in mind, there could be a conflict of interest because your actions could potentially reduce their commission check. For franchise resales, you might have to wait months if not years for the right opportunity to arise especially if you are focused on a particular industry or even one or two franchise brands.

CASE STUDY:
MARK WOODSUM
And Brightstar

Acquiring an Existing Franchise and Growing 8X

Franchise Acquired in 2015

Previous Experience: Foreign Service Officer

Franchise: BrightStar Care

BrightStar Care is a home health care franchise dedicated to providing both medical and non-medical assistance for families and individuals in need. Mark Woodsum is a franchisee of BrightStar, and his franchise alone has over 300 employees across Orange County, California. He owns four franchises himself and is the president of the BrightStar Owners Association (over 200 owners in the U.S.). With a background as an Army Ranger, foreign service officer, ordained Episcopal priest, and businessman, he has brought many talents to the franchise industry. Having a vocational interest in the elderly and earning an MBA inspired him to become a franchisee.

BrightStar has grown exponentially over the past several years. Many opportunities have existed recently with the COVID pandemic, causing many industry acquisitions lately. These franchises have been highly profitable with a significant sales track record and real income potential.

Mark has grown his business since 2015 and has had to clash with the franchisor to fight for the rights of his business operation as well as hundreds of franchisees in the BrightStar organization. While Mark started out in home health care, It is not currently his only business line. Other business lines include staffing and clinical trials.

Mark emphasized that it is a difficult business to get off the ground. Once this business is built to a certain scale, it can be quite lucrative because you are adding significant value along the way. Larger population centers like Orange County, California and regions with existing operations help shorten the time period to become a profitable enterprise. Franchise owners helping each other leads to business growth. Owners often work long hours (he commuted three hours round-trip every day at the start) and can wear three different hats; e.g., sales, operational, and medical expertise.

In terms of investment, it helped Mark to have extra capital to invest $200k to $300k, whereas the norm for BrightStar would be $150k to $200k in the first 12-18 months. It took Mark approximately a year to "turn around" an existing franchise (instead of starting from scratch) with some structural changes. He did his own research on franchises and did not use a business broker.

As president of the franchisee organization, Mark has also put in significant hours, and through his hard work he has helped everyone grow as a united force. The common goal of both the franchisees and the franchisor is "top-line revenue." The owners have to assure that monies are going to the bottom line, whereas the franchisor is less concerned with that.

He strongly urges that franchisees communicate regularly with the franchisor headquarters operation. An annual Franchise Disclosure Document and a "call option" (buy-back of a franchise) are a part of the franchisor/franchisee partnership. It is sometimes also advisable for a franchisee to buy into the franchise. A franchise agreement should recognize different types of geographical territories and include renewal options.

A place like California is pro-employee and pro-franchisee and will not recognize a non-compete clause in a franchise-related contract, so going independent is easier than in other states. But maintaining brand equity needs to be a consideration for any franchisee thinking about going independent. It is not uncommon for disagreements to arise between a franchisor and franchisee (e.g., whether to work with Medicare Advantage at BrightStar or to include a "call option" in a franchise agreement).

In addition to communication, development of a positive culture is important with a franchise so that everyone is working toward mutual success, a win-win. Empathy in understanding the other person's position leads to finding common ground.

Mark has been quite successful and lives by the maxim "Don't work in the business; work on the business." Moreover, he understands that job satisfaction is not a "one size fits all." Having the human touch at the "end of life" with his Episcopal priest background has also been helpful in his business growth.

While many hours need to be dedicated by the entrepreneurial franchisee, this lifestyle also has given Mark flexibility to dictate his own schedule (e.g., not missing a son's swim meet). "Never having a dull moment" has certainly been to Mark's advantage!

CHECKLIST

☐ Speak with at least four franchisors.

☐ Ask the franchise development representative if there are any available resales and if he can assist you in connecting with the seller.

6

RESEARCH WEEK: FRANCHISE DISCLOSURE DOCUMENT (FDD), PROFORMAS, & "DEEP DIVES"

"Research is formalized curiosity.
It is poking and prying with a purpose."

Zora Neale Hurston

As you start week six, you should start looking at the FDDs provided by the franchisors that you are considering. The FDD is a legal document that the franchisor presents to prospective franchisees in the franchise pre-sale process. Many states regulate franchising, and a few require registration to sell the franchise opportunity. The FDD is an extensive document that discloses detailed information about the franchisor and the franchise. The FDD gives the potential franchisee information on the organization to plan and help decide on their investment.

The document is divided into 23 categories, labeled as "Items." Typically, the most important items to analyze are Items 3, 4, 6, 7, 8, 9, 12, 19, 20, 21, and 22. We have taken the most important subjects for you to "deep-dive" into the FDD and other information you collect.

REVIEW PRINCIPALS, LITIGATION, AND BANKRUPTCIES

Source: Items 3 and 4 of FDD and Google

At this stage, you are excited to start your own business. The last thing you want to worry about is unethical behavior (that is publicly known) or that the very business model you are buying into is at risk of failing. Fortunately, Item 3 reviews litigation required to be disclosed by the franchisor and Item 4 reveals any bankruptcies.

Moreover, you should search on Google the first 5 pages (so 40+ results) with "FRANCHISE NAME litigation" and "FRANCHISE LEGAL NAME litigation." For example, search for "Subway litigation" and "Doctor's Associates Inc. litigation" and see what comes up. Keep in mind that some of the lawsuits might be against the franchisees by consumers, but typing in the legal name of the franchise found on Item 2 should do the trick.

Also, Google the Principals/CEO/Leadership members until the sixth Google page. Their names are included on Item 2 of the FDD.

Conduct additional searches including "lawsuit," "litigation," and "dispute" along with the relevant name(s) of the executive(s) and corporate entities.

In Google News type in "review of FRANCHISE NAME." Also browse through Yelp reviews (average rating, types of reviews) for that franchise.

A few franchises with a checkered past include Mellow Mushroom, Dental Fix RX, and Planet Beach. These franchisors have sued a former franchisee, leading to a bankruptcy. These are franchisors who are often making $1M+ a year, and they are suing a franchisee whose business failed into bankruptcy.

Now this is not illegal and they are often in line with the franchise agreement, but you can get the idea of how the franchisor will act when the franchisee is in a precarious situation. Many franchisors will simply release you from any obligations for royalty payments, etc., while others will sue you for every last penny! A former client of Visa Franchise was unable to open up his property management franchise due to health reasons. The franchisor did not require him to pay 10 years of royalties. Rather, they kept the majority of the $40,000 franchise fee and canceled the agreement.

The entire business model and branding can be at risk too! This was the case for Crest Foods, which runs Nestle Toll House Café. Crest Foods was sued by Nestle USA in 2016 over the use of their name/trademark. Nestle USA claimed the Nestle Toll House Café franchise went too far in its use of marks including when one of their executives went on CBS's Undercover Boss and pretended to be a Nestle executive.

A major reason to buy a Nestle Toll House Café, Haagen-Dazs, or Ben & Jerry's franchise is to distribute those products to customers who already know about (and often love) the brand. You are building on the success of 20, 50, or even 150+ years, as is the case with Nestle.

What are the fees and cost for starting and running a franchise?

Sources: Items 6 and 7; Vetted Biz (through comparing with other franchises)

Item 6 discloses all the fees related to the franchise, either one-time or ongoing fees, and Item 7 describes the initial costs in starting a franchise.

For Anytime Fitness (over 2,300 locations in U.S.), the franchisor earns

$200,000+ before you open up as you are buying much of the initial startup items from them directly. This includes many fees that can be required payments to Anytime Fitness.

ITEM 7.
ESTIMATED INITIAL INVESTMENT

YOUR ESTIMATED INITIAL INVESTMENT

TYPE OF EXPENDITURE (Note 1)	AMOUNT				METHOD OF PAYMENT	WHEN DUE	TO WHOM PAYMENT IS TO BE MADE
	ANYTIME FITNESS		ANYTIME FITNESS EXPRESS				
	LOW	HIGH	LOW	HIGH			
Initial Franchise/ Development Fee (Note 2)	$42,500	$42,500	$25,000	$25,000	Lump sum	When you sign your franchise agreement	Us
Travel and Training Expenses (Note 3)	$3,000	$3,500	$3,000	$3,500	As Incurred	Before and During Training	Vendors (e.g., travel, hotel, restaurants)
Deposit and Leashold Improvements (Note 4)	$7,871	$371,142	$3,832	$274,792	As Incurred	As Incurred	Third Parties
3 Months' Rent (Note 4)	$23,614	$28,116	$11,495	$12,980	As Incurred	As Incurred	Third Parties
Architect/Design Fees (Note 5)	$6,000	$16,080	$6,000	$10,950	As specified in contract	At the time of design	Architect
Fitness Equipment (Note 6)	$153,010	$153,010	$137,081	$137,081	Lump Sum	Before Issuing Order for the Equipment	Us, affiliates, or Vendors
Technology Equipment Package (Note 6)	$34,805	$36,224	$28,488	$28,488	Lump Sum	Before Issuing Order for the Equipment	Us, affiliates, or Vendors
Supplies (Note 7)	$3,575	$3,575	$3,050	$3,050	As Incurred	As Incurred	Vendors
Interior & Exterior Signs (Note 8)	$24,000	$26,000	$16,000	$18,000	Lump Sum	Before Opening	Us or Vendors
Miscellaneous Opening Costs (Note 9)	$10,000	$11,000	$8,000	$9,500	As Incurred	As Incurred	Vendors
Pre-Sale/Grand Opening Advertising (Note 10)	$11,000	$23,000	$0	$5,000	As Incurred	60 Days Before and After Opening	Us or Vendors
Insurance/Bond (Note 11)	$2,900	$3,450	$2,700	$2,700	Lump Sum	Before Opening	Vendors
Furniture & Fixtures	$13,000	$15,300	$13,000	$15,000	As Incurred	Before Opening	Vendors
Additional Funds – 3 Months (Note 12)	$46,300	$51,000	$33,100	$38,400	As Incurred	As Incurred	Suppliers, Utilities, etc.
Total (Note 13)	$381,575	$783,897	$290,746	$584,441			

Questionable fees to watch out for include:

Excessive Technology Fees

These should be mutually beneficial to both the franchisor and its franchisees. You cannot have some POS (point-of-sale) system that the franchisor develops and is inferior to other options on the market. For example, Anytime Fitness charges a $799 monthly base technology fee while other franchise systems charge in excess of $1,500.

Understand how much the franchisor is making off you in addition to the clean, straightforward franchise fee. Use basic math on how much the franchisor (royalty fee percentage and franchise fee) makes from the franchisee.

Marketing and Advertisement Fee

The advertising fund contributed by franchisees can range from 0% to 4% of the total cost. The franchisor might not always raise funds for advertising, but most FDDs allow for this in Item 6. These funds should be segregated and kept in a separate account from other checking accounts held by the franchisor.

The funds should be used for promoting the products and services offered by the franchisees in the system to the customers of the business.

A franchisor should provide franchisees with an annual accounting of the fund. Also, if the franchisor operates company-owned locations, they should make contributions to the advertising fund at the same rate as franchisees are required to make.

Working Capital: Funds Needed Once Business Opens

How much additional capital do you need to invest in the business until you break even and you are able to start taking dividends out of the business or even paying yourself? Many franchisors will disclose in Item 7 all the expenses, including working capital or additional capital. Some choose to be conservative and give an estimate of whether it is a six-month or nine-month timeline for the amount of capital needed to sustain the business to break even. Other franchisors will just list three months of working capital, which according to our research at Vetted Biz is not enough time to break even, and you're probably going to have to inject additional capital.

In addition to working capital, another important consideration is how many hours that franchisees work in the business. This relates directly to income and the return on your time invested in the business. It goes beyond the capital you have injected into the business. Consequently, you must obtain this type of information directly by speaking with multiple franchisees (in step 8).

Capital Expenditures: Updating Furniture, Fixtures, and Equipment.

Most businesses require an update three to five years after you first open. On the low end it could be replacing a computer, and on the high end it could be spending $50,000+ on new exercise equipment for your gym franchise.

Frequency and cost limits should be included in the franchise agreement. It is important to confirm what you are legally obliged to do and what the franchisor has done in practice.

SOURCING GOODS AND SERVICES...WHAT ABOUT REBATES?

Item 8 details the franchisee's obligations to purchase or source goods, services, and supplies from specific suppliers. It also details whether the franchisor is currently receiving rebates or is allowed to receive rebates from the suppliers.

The franchisor should foster the economies of scale associated with group purchasing to benefit its franchisees across the system. A franchisee should have the right to purchase from any supplier who meets the franchisor's reasonable and necessary standards and specifications.

Occasionally the franchisees derive most of the value with group purchasing. This is the case for Subway franchisees who have an independent co-op separate from the franchisor that negotiates prices in bulk for most supplies/food needed for a Subway restaurant. On the other end of the scale, a cell phone repair franchisee must buy specific products from the franchisor, which may be sourced from alternative vendors for less money and better quality.

What happens when you want to sell the business or have an issue?

Item 9 contains information on renewal rights, non-compete and confidentiality requirements, termination rights, and legal forum selection provisions.

Resale values can be obtained through our company, Vetted Biz. Resale values can also be obtained on BizBuySell and other business-for-sale websites. (You should apply a 10% cut as businesses usually close for less than the asking price.)

Franchisees should have the right to renew the franchise agreement for specified periods of time (generally the agreement is for 10 to 20 years).

The franchisor will charge a transfer fee 99% of the time. This fee should be significantly lower than your initial franchise fee, and it should go toward training costs and legal costs.

Resale or transfer fees should not pad profits for a franchisor, as has been the case with Dickey's BBQ and Snap-on.

If a transfer is to a current franchisee, then the transfer fee should be less (or waived) than if the transfer is to a new franchisee.

Some franchises, like F45 fitness, keep the true transfer fee cost vague; legal and accounting fees could easily surpass another $10,000.

Below, you can see a selection of ongoing fees taken from Item 6 on F45 Fitness' 2022 FDD.

F45 TRAINING

Type of Fee	Amount
Royalty Fee	The greater of 7% of Gross Sales(2) or $2,500 per month
Marketing Fee	$2,500 per month
Service Fee	Currently, $500 per month
Transfer Fee	25% of the then-current establishment fee, plus our reasonable costs and expenses associated with the transfer, including training costs and legal and accounting fees

When you think of the total cost of the franchise, you should include the transfer fee as this fee is essentially absorbed by you as the seller. If someone has the opportunity to buy one of two property management businesses with similar financials, a transfer fee of $0 or $30,000 could make the difference for the buyer.

When the franchise agreement ends (because of the term or sale), the franchisee ideally should not be prohibited from continuing in the same type of business, but this is rarely the case. Generally, you have to negotiate this clause before signing the franchise agreement, or with less bargaining power when you choose to leave the franchise system.

There can be measures that restrict the confidential information and trade secrets of the franchisor. However, if someone has always worked in education and they buy a franchise in education that does not work out, they should be able to continue working in that field (whether as a manager or owner).

CASE STUDY:

NATE COOMBS

Is a Second-Generation Franchisee and Continuing to Grow

Franchise Opened in 2004

Previous Experience: Military and Construction

Franchise: DreamMaker Kitchen & Bath

It is important that the franchisee and the franchisor share the same core values, especially when it comes to treating customers fairly.

Being the trusted professional remodeler choice is the goal for this franchise.

In Nate's case, his father had an architectural firm and he wanted to expand into remodeling. This was a second business for his father. Nate worked in the family business and eventually took over operations a few years back.

A franchisee who wants to open and break even fast with substantial income in the near term must have the right set-up. For instance, having 12 months of operating capital for a year, help with marketing from the franchiser, expert accounting advice, and financial support for administrative staff are all useful. DreamMaker franchisees receive substantial training from the franchisor. All this helps set the foundation for strong, stable, and profitable growth, performed with excellence.

During the COVID pandemic, business actually grew for Nate because people were staying home and they decided to remodel and update. While Nate is backed up with business, it is critical to order projects as soon as a customer contract is signed.

Nate has nine full-time employees that cover sales, administrative support, and the contractor work. Project managers work with the trade partners in conjunction with the design team from start to finish.

Before Nate joined the military years ago, he had some construction and architectural firm experience. So when he left the military it was natural for him to join his father's business because they shared the same values. Nate's military background has helped him work with systems in place and checklists.

Nate's typical work week is Monday through Friday (8-5) overseeing sales and office management. He does not work nights or weekends. This has resulted in a high quality of life. Nate is a businessman who enjoys spending time with his family.

At least half of Nate's business comes from referrals or past customers. The rest comes from marketing, especially on the internet.

In 2021, the average DreamMaker location did $1,451,000 in business, a solid figure. So the average franchisee is performing in the top 5% in the industry. DreamMaker is one of the top home service franchises in the country. Investment and performance are interconnected. To build a bigger business, oftentimes a higher amount of capital needs to be injected.

Franchisees come in with investments through a variety of ways, including SBA loans or 401(k) conversions or a combination of both.

One of the markets for expansion is Texas, given all the Californians moving there. In Nate's case, he is seeing people moving to Utah with money to be able to update their homes.

At the outset of a project, Nate likes to invite his clients to see their design center as well as different products and materials. Meeting people in person is always preferable to online discussions (as seen with COVID).

Their business has returned to their pre-COVID in-person meetings.

Besides having a shared code of values, assuring the right fit with people and following systems are essential for success. Nate emphasized the importance of quality of life as well as the overall support received from the DreamMaker franchise.

FRANCHISE TERRITORY

Item 12 contains details on the exclusivity of the franchisee's territory. This is one of the key terms that is open to negotiation in most franchise systems. You can paint a roadmap to the franchisor for expanding in your area and asking for right of first refusal for adjacent territory. Also, the protective territory – whether by radius, zip code, or population size – might be open for negotiation. Do all you can not to set yourself up for competing with franchisees in your market. There is enough competition in most industries and markets to worry about besides your own franchisee peers.

FINANCIALS PERFORMANCE OF FRANCHISEES

Item 19 discloses financial performance representations. Franchisors should be required to disclose financials, but this is still optional. Less than 60% of franchisors disclose gross revenue figures, and they disclose even less figures like operating costs and net income before taxes.

Currently, financial performance provided by the franchisor (or outsourced sales firm) must be disclosed in Item 19. This creates a more cumbersome but necessary process of vetting the information (or lack of information) with franchisees to see what their sales and profits have been.

While Teriyaki Madness advertises a average unit volume (AUV) of $1.16 million, this reflects just 36% of all their locations. You only discover this by reading the fine print from Item 19 of the FDD.

TERIYAKI MADNESS FRANCHISE OWNERS
HAVE HUGE BOWLS AND BIG PROFITS

We don't mind bragging; we're ranked among the most profitable food franchises. On average, here's how things shake out:

AVERAGE UNIT VOLUME
(AUV)

STACKED SAME SHOP SALES GROWTH
(2021 vs. 2019)

$1.16
MILLION

32%
GROWTH

Our Average Unit Volume (AUV) is $1,161,201*. Find out more about your earnings potential in our Franchise Disclosure Document (FDD), which includes the Item 19 that shows Income Statements from Teriyaki Madness franchisees. Item 19 can help you understand potential revenue, labor costs, COGS and profit margins.

There are more than 125 Teriyaki Madness shops open across the United States including two in Mexico and two in Canada! With strong support, numbers and scalability, TMAD is a fantastic addition to your franchise portfolio or a great choice for first-time franchisees.

November 2021: https://franchise.teriyakimadness.com/franchise-profitability/

Year	High Gross Sales	Low Gross Sales	Average Gross Sales ("AGS")	Number of Teriyaki Shops at or above AGS	Percentage of Teriyaki Shops at or above AGS	Median Gross Sales ("MGS")	Number of Teriyaki Shops at or above MGS	Percentage of Teriyaki Shops at or above MGS
2021	$2,275,568	$525,289	$1,161,201	17	47%	$1,101,124	18	50%
2020	$1,666,686	$508,366	$1,079,488	10	45%	$1,071,902	11	50%
2019	$1,564,146	$720,371	$1,154,180	8	53%	$1,183,295	8	53%
2018	$1,430,790	$631,431	$1,134,507	7	54%	$1,247,256	7	54%
2017	$1,338,244	$585,002	$1,079,140	6	60%	$1,126,762	6	55%
2016	$1,405,107	$645,613	$1,148,596	5	56%	$1,179,139	5	56%

Gross Sales Table*

* Teriyaki Shops owned by our Predecessor's affiliate do not pay a Royalty Fee but do contribute Marketing Fund Contributions. These Teriyaki Shops are included in the 2016, 2017, 2018, 2019, 2020 and 2021 data.

Notes to Gross Sales Table:

1. "Gross Sales" means the revenues received from the sale of food, beverages, services and other items from in-store dining, carry-out, online orders, delivery, third party voucher sales, catering, and otherwise, including the sale of food and beverages, redemption of gift cards, and merchandise and all other income and consideration of every kind and nature related to the Teriyaki Madness Business or Teriyaki Madness Business operations (including all proceeds from any business interruption insurance) whether for cash or credit and regardless of collection in the case of credit, but does not include any sales taxes or other taxes collected from customers for, and thereafter paid directly to, the appropriate taxing authority.

2. As of December 31, 2021, we had 100 franchised Teriyaki Shops. The information in the table above is a historical financial performance representation for the 36 franchised Teriyaki Shops that met the Conditions. Sixty-four Teriyaki Shops did not meet this requirement and were not included. Forty-three were not open for at least two years, five were smaller than 1,350 square feet, two were larger than 3,000 square feet, one was in a non-traditional space, nine had a change of franchisee ownership within the two-year period, and four are currently for sale.

3. As of December 31, 2020, we had 88 franchised Teriyaki Shops. The information in the table above is a historical financial performance representation for the 22 franchised Teriyaki Shops that met the Conditions. Sixty-six Teriyaki Shops did not meet this requirement and were not included. Forty-eight were not open for at least two years, five were smaller than 1,350 square feet, two were larger than 3,000 square feet, two were in a non-traditional space, and nine had a change of franchisee ownership within the two-year period.

Smoothie King follows a similar approach. In the advertisement below, they claim a 20% Average EBITDA on $907,000 of AUV. These numbers only reflect the top 25% of franchisees, and the ad discloses this in a minuscule-size font in the ad.

Luckily, the Item 19 (shown below) is more forthcoming and shows the true picture of AUV being $609,000. That is a $300,000 difference from the advertised AUV!

Table 19-1 Average Net Sales of USA Units
December 29, 2020 to December 27, 2021

	Top 10%	Top 25%	Top 50%	Top 75%	TOTAL (ALL)
Number of Units in Category	88	220	440	660	880
Average Net Sales	$1,062,545	$907,346	$775,979	$689,233	$609,753
Number and Percent that Met or Exceeded the Average Net Sales in Category	36/41%	84/38%	176/40%	266/40%	377/43%
Median Net Sales	$1,014,225	$855,618	$730,050	$643,696	$573,269
Range of Net Sales (high)	$1,605,120	$1,605,120	$1,605,120	$1,605,120	$1,605,120
Range of Net Sales (low)	$896,948	$730,074	$573,792	$461,013	$156,243
	Bottom 10%	Bottom 25%	Bottom 50%	Bottom 75%	TOTAL (ALL)
Number of Units in Category	88	220	440	660	880
Average Net Sales	$304,367	$371,310	$443,526	$510,555	$609,753
Number and Percent that Met or Exceeded the Average Net Sales in Category	50/57%	124/56%	247/56%	339/51%	377/43%
Median Net Sales	$313,983	$385,209	$460,896	$514,148	$573,269
Range of Net Sales (high)	$363,472	$460,778	$572,747	$730,026	$1,605,120
Range of Net Sales (low)	$156,243	$156,243	$156,243	$156,243	$156,243

American Freight takes an even more aggressive stance by disclosing AUV of less than 10% of their company owned and operated locations (only 20 stores in total) in the below advertisement.

AMERICAN FREIGHT
FURNITURE · MATTRESS · APPLIANCE

EASY TO BUILD
QUICK TO OPEN
HIGHLY SCALABLE

LET'S CUT TO THE BOTTOM LINE

AVERAGE GROSS SALES PER STORE*
$5,590,180
AVERAGE NET INCOME PER STORE*
$1,006,555

· Built for multi-unit growth
· Turnkey setup, systems and support
· 360+ store buying power
· Established and growing company

American Freight has 42 stores with an AUV of $1.1 million as shown in Table 1-A of their 2022 FDD. I wonder why they did not lead with those numbers...

TABLE 1-A

Statement of Average Revenues and Expenses
For American Freight Company-Operated Businesses
Opened 12 Months or More for Fiscal Year 2021 (by Revenue Range)

	Gross Sales Below $1.50M		Gross Sales Between $1.5M - $2.49M		Gross Sales Between $2.5M - $3.49M		Gross Sales Between $3.5M - $4.5M		Gross Sales Over $4.5M	
	Average	%	Average	%	Average	%	Average	%	Average	%
Gross Sales (Note 1)	$1,131,901	100.0%	$1,985,394	100.0%	$3,044,787	100.0%	$3,966,446	100.0%	$5,590,180	100.0%
Total COGS (Note 2)	$626,530	55.4%	$1,153,157	58.1%	$1,721,227	56.5%	$2,232,998	56.3%	$3,122,759	55.9%
Gross Profit (Note 3)	$505,371	44.6%	$832,237	41.9%	$1,323,560	43.5%	$1,733,448	43.7%	$2,467,421	44.1%
Expenses										
Royalty Fee (Note 4)	$56,595	5.0%	$99,270	5.0%	$152,239	5.0%	$198,322	5.0%	$279,509	5.0%
Wages - (Note 5)	$174,854	15.4%	$251,141	12.6%	$351,955	11.6%	$455,690	11.5%	$604,539	10.8%
Occupancy Expenses (Note 6)	$207,381	18.3%	$240,888	12.1%	$223,333	7.3%	$250,912	6.3%	$302,243	5.4%
Advertising Expense (Note 7)	$85,541	7.6%	$93,927	4.7%	$93,734	3.1%	$118,199	3.0%	$145,760	2.6%
Miscellaneous Expenses (Note 8)	$49,026	4.3%	$61,704	3.1%	$76,104	2.5%	$88,327	2.2%	$110,815	2.0%
Technology Fee (Note 9)	$18,000	1.6%	$18,000	0.9%	$18,000	0.6%	$18,000	0.5%	$18,000	0.3%
Total Expense (Note 10)	$591,397	52.2%	$764,930	38.5%	$915,366	30.1%	$1,129,450	28.5%	$1,460,866	26.1%
Net Income (Note 11)	($86,026)	-7.6%	$67,307	3.4%	$408,194	13.4%	$603,998	15.2%	$1,006,555	18.0%
Number of Stores In Sample	42		68		32		28		20	
Avg Age of Stores in Sample	1 - 9 years		1 - 27 years		1 - 27 years		3 - 25 years		2 - 20 years	

Other Item 19s speak for themselves, like the one for Crumbl Cookies. Their straightforward presentation sells itself, and I have yet to see them advertise their financials or appear on any "best franchise list" like the *Entrepreneur 500*. With an average net profit of $357,000, you can open the business for as little as $300,000? Few franchises that have a physical buildout have financials like Crumbl.

From Crumbl's 2022 FDD:

FRANCHISE LOCATION AVERAGE PERFORMANCE

The representation made below is an historic financial performance representation of a subset of Crumbl® locations that operated continuously through all of 2021. The total number of franchised outlets that existed at the beginning of 2021 and operated continuously through 2021 was 140, which equates to approximately 43.11% of the total franchised locations that were operating at the end of 2021. 25 of these stores did not timely submit their final and complete financial data as of the issuance date of this disclosure document and are not included in this data set. The following data represents the average, high, median, and low 2021 calendar year financial data for such 115 Crumbl® locations. The chart shows the Total Revenue, Gross Profit, Gross Margin, Net Profit, and Net Margin (defined below) for the 2021 Calendar year from such locations. These locations operated in several states across the United States. These locations serve the same type of goods that you will be serving. These locations are each within territories of approximately 40,000 to 125,000 people. Your location will likely face different competition, costs, customer preferences, population numbers, and other factors.

2021 Calendar Year	Average	High	Median	Low
Total Revenue	$1,687,731	$3,639,139	$1,582,090	$734,278
Gross Profit	$749,555	$1,771,793	$707,912.53	$282,380
Net Profit	$357,512	$618,102	$279,212	$33,260

Beware of emerging franchise concepts (started franchising within the last three years and/or less than 20 locations open) that only show financials for their affiliate/corporate locations. Generally, the franchisor has 10-20+ years of industry experience and knows the business intimately. Especially while the founder is still involved in the franchise system, the affiliate locations will often have average sales 20%+ higher than franchised locations. This revenue bump can have a major impact on the bottom line financials; i.e., the money you take home from the business.

OPENINGS, CLOSURES, AND MORE!

Item 20 discloses a list of franchise outlets.

Franchise failures comprise franchise terminations, franchise non-renewals, and franchises that ceased operations for other reasons. All of these metrics are accessible in Item 20.

You can also see if the franchise system has net unit growth or net loss in units. Take 2021 for instance, Subway had a net loss of 1,500 restaurants in a single year!

You compare that with Sign Gypsies, which has opened up hundreds of locations with few failures. That being said, net growth is easier for emerging brands than for franchisors that have been around for 20+ years.

For franchise systems with high net unit growth, you must vet how the franchisor supports franchisees during your conversations with franchisees.

FINANCIAL PERFORMANCE OF FRANCHISOR

Item 21 discloses the income statement, cash flow, and balance sheet of the franchisor for the last few years.

This is probably one of the best yet most overlooked resources for figuring out the health of a franchise brand. Use these franchisor disclosures to your advantage!

If the parent company is publicly traded there will be even more information in their quarterly and annual reports. However, 95%+ of franchisors are privately owned and not traded on the stock market.

The franchisor could be owned by a private equity fund, founder, and/or other investment group. It is important to assess why and how much they are investing.

Understand what is riding on the performance of their franchise system (including franchisees making money!). Would they mortgage their home to make the franchise brand work like you are willing to do?

Or are they making millions of dollars a year and reinvesting the profits back into the business? The income statement, taken from the 2022 FDD of Real Property Management owned by Neighborly, shows a profitable franchisor. Most of the income is derived from servicing current franchisees not selling to new franchisees.

Neighborly Assetco LLC and Subsidiaries

Combined Statements of Income
($000's)

	September 1, 2021 through December 31, 2021 (Successor)		March 26, 2021 through August 31, 2021 (Predecessor)
Revenues and income			
Franchise service fees	$	46,350	$ 64,679
Synthetic royalties and master license fees		4,482	8,958
Franchise sales fees		3,705	6,580
Sales of products and services		7,157	21,133
Advertising and promotional fund revenue		12,045	13,431
Interest and other		10,473	11,095
Total revenues and income		84,212	125,876
Cost of products and services		4,934	11,372
Gross Profit		79,278	114,504
Selling expense		1,676	2,522
Advertising and promotional fund expense		12,045	13,431
Amortization		25,454	5,637
Management expenses		10,206	13,123
Bad debt expense		413	157
Net income	$	29,484	$ 79,634

On the other extreme is BurgerIM (fast casual restaurant), which sold over a thousand locations with barely a proof of concept in the United States. In their December 31, 2018 balance sheet taken from the 2019 FDD, BurgerIM had minimal assets including $53,000 in cash and a Porshe Cayenne on the balance sheet.

BURGERIM GROUP USA, INC.
BALANCE SHEET
DECEMBER 31, 2018

ASSETS

Current assets	
Cash	$ 53,304
Franchise fees receivable	5,634,717
Employee advances	10,358
Total current assets	5,698,379
Property and equipment	
Office equipment	60,136
Furniture and fixtures	43,488
Vehicle	71,302
	174,926
Less accumulated depreciation	<108,411>
Total property and equipment	66,515
Other assets	
Prepaid R & D Expenses	1,299,085
Loans to Franchises	331,544
Intangible assets	200,000
Security deposit	14,711
	1,845,340
Total assets	$ 7,610,234

In their December 31, 2018 Income Statement, 99% of BurgerIM's income was generated through the sale of new franchise licenses. This is a major red flag as BurgerIM should have been more focused on helping existing franchisees grow their restaurant sales. Through increased restaurant sales the franchisor would have generated more royalty income. Be mindful when franchisors earn most of their revenue from selling franchises not serving existing franchisees.

FRANCHISE AGREEMENT AND OTHER DOCUMENTS YOU SIGN

Item 22 contains a list of all the legal agreements and contracts attached to the FDD. The franchise agreement is the main agreement, but leases, options, financing agreements, and purchase agreements may also apply.

We will review this in more detail during week 11 (negotiating; signing franchise agreement with franchise attorney guidance).

Be sure to understand the potential liabilities for you as a franchisee. You might be liable not only for the lease should you close the business but unpaid royalties and other payments due to the franchisor.

CREATING A BASIC FINANCIAL MODEL (PROFORMA)

Now, based on information collected from Items 7 and 19 of the FDD, you can start inputting financial assumptions into a proforma for the franchise business.

Lean on the finance specialist or bank lender to see if they have already supported financing with this system or with a similar concept. They might have a sample template to share with you or at least advise if you are headed in the right direction with your assumptions before conversations with the franchisor and franchisees.

The franchisor will have a proforma but might be hesitant to offer it to you for liability reasons. It doesn't hurt to ask the franchisor as well as franchisees in their system for proformas.

You can opt to retain an accountant to assist in the preparation of a business plan with five-year financial projections.

CHECKLIST

☐ Check for any litigation matters involving the franchise.

☐ Learn to differentiate proper fees from questionable ones.

☐ Beware of the fine print.

7

DEEP DIVE CALLS WITH FRANCHISORS

"Trust, but verify."

Ronald Reagan

You are now in week 7 and more than halfway through the process. This week, you are going to dive deeper into the franchises that are on your short list. You should now start to review your findings from the FDDs and the information packages the franchisors sent you. This is also a good time to start reaching out to any franchisees of the companies to learn more about their business from the knowledge lens you now have. It can take time to schedule these calls, and you need to start once the franchise brand is a serious option for you.

Once you further narrow down some potential businesses, start conversations with the franchisor about where you would open your store, restaurant, or service. This will help make better sense of your financial projections. Real estate will be a major cost consideration when you are starting a franchise.

In case you have not covered questions below in earlier conversations with the franchisor, you must have these answered before moving past week 7.

1. Can you give me a breakdown of all the expenses associated with getting started?

2. Explain the contractual responsibilities if I join your franchise system (i.e., length of the agreement, renewals, etc.).

How long is it for? Do you have to pay another franchise fee, half a franchise fee, or nothing if you want to renew after five or 10 years? Are you able to buy products and services from any vendor, or do they have to be pre-approved? How does the franchisor make money beyond the royalties? Are they making money in other ways, beyond the initial franchise fee, in addition to the royalties they collect?

3. What does your training program look like? What ongoing training do you offer?

What franchise executives and manager will you be interacting with on a daily/weekly basis throughout the franchise license? Who will be your key point of contact, and will you be assigned a franchise coach?

4. What is my protected territory and how is it defined?

5. Is there collective purchasing power with suppliers?

Do all discounts with suppliers pass through to franchisees, or are there rebates received by the franchisor? There might even be an independent co-op (rare but possible) as is the case for Subway. In an independent co-op, franchisees negotiate pricing directly with the suppliers, and generally the franchisor is not involved and does not receive any monetary benefit.

5. To be direct, how many franchised units have failed and why?

6. How have previous franchisee-franchisor disputes been settled?

If after two years, I have worked 40-60+ hours a week and the business does not make money, what happens?

7. What happens when I want to retire or sell my business?

CHECKLIST

☐ Reach out to franchisees.

☐ Decide which franchisor to continue evaluating.

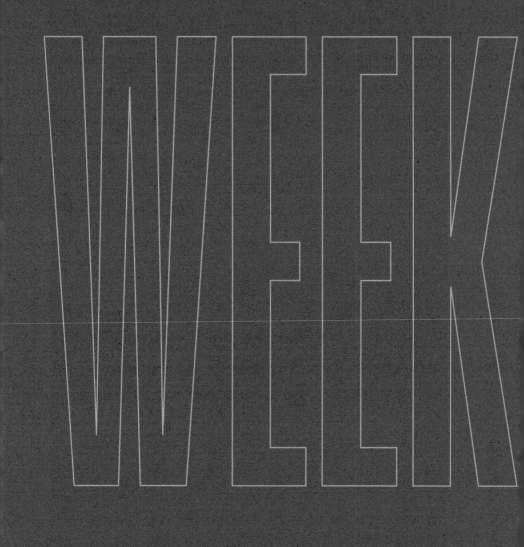

8

VALIDATE INFORMATION COLLECTED WITH FRANCHISEES

"Trust is built with consistency."

Lincoln Chafee

"Knowledge is power. The real test of knowledge is not whether it is true but whether it empowers us."

Sir Francis Bacon

During this week, will start contacting the franchisees we recommended earlier. However, if you have not started yet, it is not too late. Franchisees will always be able to help you get a better sense of what the business will look like for you. They might also be able to help you with information that you did not obtain from the company itself.

Franchisees in your area will also help you understand better how your identified region would respond to a certain business. For example, a restaurant that does well in Manhattan might not do as well in rural Alabama. This is a crucial step because the franchisor will usually provide you with the data for your entire system, which might be different when localized to your area of operations.

Try to speak with 10 franchisees including at least two franchisees who have left the system. The ones who have left will help you understand the downsides of the business – the only caveat is that occasionally the ones that left just wanted to retire or had some other reason not necessarily related to the business.

If you are still having trouble connecting after reaching out three times, you can offer to compensate franchisees with a $50 or $100 Amazon gift card. Best to ask for 20-30 minutes to connect. It is difficult to ask a franchisee to allocate a full hour to your investigation especially if they are not being compensated.

Share the Proforma you created as a Google doc. Ask for insights into the numbers on the call, whether you are on the right track or if there is anything they would adjust. You can ask if they would be willing to share their proforma and/or actual financials.

While on a call with current franchisees, ask leading questions that will get them to open up. Some examples might include: What is the actual working capital to break even? What is your main function on a typical day? How many hours do you work?

Additional questions to ask:

- How long have you been a franchisee?

- Have you always worked these hours or was it only after the business hit critical mass?

- Can you share some information on the financials – e.g., sales, profit? Similar to the proforma I shared? Anything you would change?

- Do you have any plans to expand into new territories?

- If you had to do it again, would you start or buy this franchise?

- Is there anything else that you would like to share with me, or that you think might help me?

- Would you recommend this franchise to others?

- What are the biggest challenges you have faced as a franchisee?

- What has been your experience with the franchisor's marketing efforts?

They might have some items that they did not want to offer up but feel obliged to tell a prospective franchisee signing a 10-year agreement!

It is possible that at the end of this process you find that the business does not suit you. That is the whole reason we are recommending a 12-week program. It is better to find a business that does not work for you at the outset, rather than when you have $1 million or $2 million invested down the road.

Former franchisees might be reluctant to share any information at all. Full disclosure of a franchisee's experience is not required depending on how the franchisee left the system. The franchisee might have signed a "gag clause," or a "covenant not to disclose."

You should ask the franchisor if there are (and if so, how many) current or former franchisees who will not be able to share information.

This step will help you weed out the bad franchises from the good ones. If you end up having too many "red flags" after talking to existing or former franchisees, you should go back to the drawing board and look at other options.

These are just some of the questions you might want to ask. You can also ask about specific concerns you have or areas you want more information about.

CHECKLIST

☐ Understand the unit level profitability of franchisees.

☐ Figure out the timeline to break even and reach expected income level.

☐ Can you picture yourself in the franchisee's shoes?

9 MARKET RESEARCH FOR YOUR AREA

"Location matters when it comes to business. Whether it's physically or virtually or both, it's important to have a presence where your clientele are present..."

Hendrith Vanlon Smith Jr.

"Location is the key to most businesses, and the entrepreneurs typically build their reputation at a particular spot."

Phyllis Schlafly

This week, you need to decide on your market and whether it is ready to receive your business. You should talk to local businesses in potential neighborhoods, strip malls, and offices where you would like to open. You should strike up casual conversations and ease into it to figure out how local businesses are doing. This is a solid strategy to obtain estimates and projections for your earnings potential.

Knowing businesses in your area that are successful will be key to understanding which industries thrive in your target market. There should be plenty of areas where foot traffic and car traffic can make it work with the local rent levels. For example, in Miami Beach, in the vicinity of 5th and Washington, there is a constant turnover in businesses while there are significant vacancies on Lincoln Road. Opening a business in Miami Beach, especially in certain areas, is a high-risk endeavor. Rents are sky-high, and only the most profitable businesses can sustain success.

Miami Beach is quite different from Houston, Texas where I saw few lease signs in similar districts. There seems to be much more room for retail districts and not the same reliance on foot traffic as Miami Beach.

A coffee franchisee in Miami was close to executing a lease for a prime location in a high-foot-traffic area. With one location already up and running with great success, the franchisee was eager to continue his growth. However, he decided to pay another visit to the location, this time not during the busy Saturday afternoon when his realtor brought him to the site.

This particular neighborhood is in the Wynwood area of Miami, mostly a weekend/ night destination. There are not too many pedestrians throughout the day from Monday through Friday. After speaking with business owners and managers of shops/restaurants in the immediate vicinity of the site, he discovered sales volume was not very high. Paying $10,000 a month rent for a coffee shop would need to produce at least $100,000 in monthly sales. Rent should be no more than 10% of sales, and for many restaurant owners in the area it was 15% or higher.

The coffee franchisee decided to focus on his existing operation and explore locations that had a more captive audience (e.g., airport or school) for his next site.

CASE STUDY:

DANIEL KRAFT

National site selection service

Finding and securing lease sites for your franchise

Daniel Kraft headed up real estate and site selection for a national retailer and has experience with construction, property management, lease negotiation, and growth. As the founder and president of National Site Selection Service, he has – for over 25 years – structured over 1,000 leases, including 700 for franchises.

One of the major challenges for franchisees is understanding the motivations of the other side, which impacts the negotiation process. For the landlord and the real estate broker, the commercial project is seen as purely an investment to maximize returns and minimize risk, whereas the franchisee oftentimes approaches the negotiations emotionally. In the franchisee's interaction with the landlord and listing agent, they should be succinct and professional while at the same time only offering the information to the landlord that is pertinent. Budget and other properties of interest are not something that should be shared with the landlord or listing agent.

The listing broker has a written agreement with the landlord. His function is to negotiate the best terms for the landlord, not the franchisee. The landlord normally wants to know how the franchisee's use could impact his other tenants (e.g., excessive parking required for the business) and what experience the franchisee has to offer. The landlord also wants to assure that the franchisee is well capitalized and wants to be sure that regular rent is coming despite fluctuations in the franchisee's business.

Honesty and transparency from the franchisee go a long way with the landlord.

Regardless of the type of landlord (e.g., real estate investment trust), whether it is discounted rent, allowances, or rental abatement, the "effective rent" – which factors all of those – is what matters. Depending on the landlord, improvements may also be part of the lease deal.

It is important for the franchisee to obtain market intelligence from the franchisor so they can understand the demographic profile of their customers. A good source is sometimes the franchisor who may have support material that will help with the site selection process. The franchisee needs to visit the site a number of times, at different hours of the day, to learn about noise levels, parking, etc.... It is important to take your time as a franchisee and have issues identified in the lease that may need to be addressed by the landlord.

If you plan on conducting due diligence on the potential commercial neighbors, please make sure to not interfere with their businesses. A good option might be having a friend ask questions for you in a discreet manner.

With respect to lease negotiations and lease review, hiring a real estate attorney with real estate leasing experience is advisable.

Regarding personal guarantees, the landlord wants to know that you are "all in on this business" and wants to be assured that the franchisee is serious. Trust is important.

Whether the landlord is a wealthy individual or an institutional investor will determine which terms the landlord will be flexible with. Many institutional investors may have deep pockets and may offer the tenant improvement cash or rental abatement as opposed to discounted rent. A local individual landlord might not have deep pockets but may be more flexible on discounted rent. During the COVID pandemic, a number of companies that might have gone out of business were given a lifeline through government payouts (for example, Paycheck Protection Program (PPP) loans). In the future, as these funds are depleted, some of these businesses may not survive. This could lead to more vacancies that a prospective franchisee might identify as a desirable location.

Due diligence is essential on whether your business use is allowed by the City for that specific area. Moreover, be cognizant of construction and power costs for your operation. It is recommended that the franchisee take their time, and take advantage of the expertise of contractors and real estate attorneys.

Through Vetted Biz, potential franchisees are given commercial real estate and financial data so that the decision becomes less emotional – even if it takes more time. This is the approach recommended by Daniel and National Site Selection Service.

COMPETITORS – YELP AND GOOGLE

Competition matters. It can serve as an indicator that there are consumers in a certain market that desire a certain product/service. For example, if there were just one ice cream shop in my college town, Waterville, Maine, there just might not be enough customers for ice cream there. Even worse, if there were not a single ice cream shop in a town with 15,000+ potential customers, there might be underlying reasons why there is none located there (weather/ employment issues, etc).

Competition can help educate the consumer of a product/service offered in a local market. If you were the first home care business to offer your service in your town, you might have to spend significant hours and money educating elderly patients and hospitals about your offering. If the customer referral sources already know about your service from a similar competitor or vendor, you can focus on differentiating your product or service instead of educating them on the need for it.

Yelp and Google serve as helpful tools for surveying competitors in the area you plan to open. If you are interested in opening a mosquito franchise, simply Google what a customer might search – "Mosquito Control near me" or "Pest Control near me" – and see what businesses pop up.

Online research is especially important for service businesses that support the customer onsite and not at their office. You might not Google "coffee shop" unless you are on vacation, but you might Google "dog day care" to see what businesses offer this service in your area. An ice cream shop or coffee shop caters to many customers looking for a quick purchase or geographically captive customers who are in an office building (coffee shop) or cluster of restaurants (ice cream shop). Moreover, you will see more people working with their laptops in a coffee shop like Starbucks than at an ice cream shop!

Some industries are localized with rent, labor, and other factors affecting the profit margin for your business. The franchisor and franchisees might not know how profitable you might be in a specific area if you are the first franchisee to open (especially the first in a metropolitan area or even a state). It is important to benchmark key profit margin and sales data across industries. At Vetted Biz, we have collected data on hundreds of business industries/categories to provide a picture, but it must be adjusted on a local level.

You should review profit and loss statements for businesses for sale in your area as well as talk with entrepreneurs about local labor costs and fluctuations that could affect your business. Labor costs in New York City are going to be drastically different than in Syracuse, New York. However, the sales volumes might not fluctuate at the same rate.

There are certain franchises that have entered cities and states and lacked the brand recognition and local market know-how to thrive. Be on the lookout for closures in your industry. On Yelp, you can even see businesses that have closed.

On Google Maps, businesses will often mark the location as temporarily closed when in fact they are permanently closed. This was the case for F45 Fitness Franchises in the Washington, D.C. area. Figure out if they are closing due to a surplus of fitness options or for other reasons such as the recent COVID pandemic.

CHECKLIST

☐ Make sure the rent for your desired location is no more than 10% of projected sales.

☐ Create a list of items in the lease that need to be addressed with the landlord.

☐ Find out if your business is allowed to operate in that location.

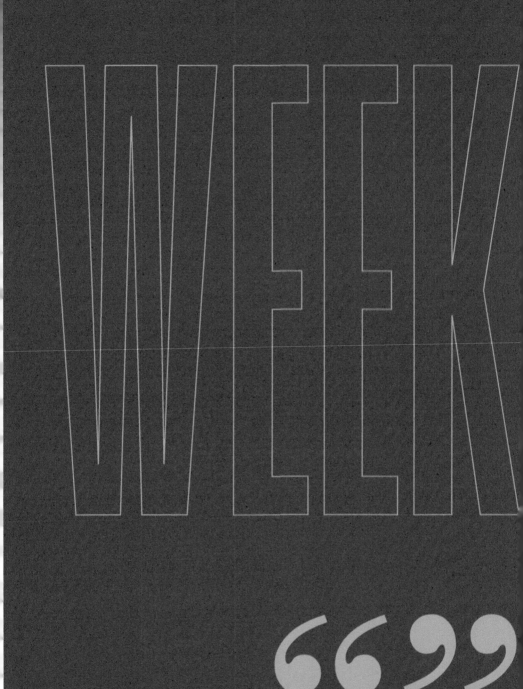

10

SECURE
FINANCING

"The desire of gold is not for gold. It is for the means of freedom and benefit."

Ralph Waldo Emerson

Now, it is time to either circle back to the financing consultant or your bank lender. You should now finalize the loan application and any other information you need to secure your financing.

Did you open up your LLC or C-Corp? Have you decided with your CPA the best structure to maximize the fiscal benefit of the business? All of these questions and more depend on what you are looking to gain from the business in the short term and long term (with a potential exit).

Make sure you have a business bank account set up. It can take a few days to receive the Employer Identification Number (EIN), also known as a Federal Tax Identification Number. This is vital for opening a business bank account and for filing payroll, federal income taxes, etc.

Moving onto the next step, if financing is taking a long time to secure, you might need to have the franchise agreement made contingent upon receiving financing from your lender. Never sign an agreement where you commit money that you do not have yet without an exit ramp.

CASE STUDY:
KRISTIN SELMECZY
And Molly Maid

Set your goals but adapt to changing circumstances while bringing in the best employees an owner can find

Franchised Started in 2007

Previous Experience: Retail Executive

Franchise: Molly Maid

As a Molly Maid franchisee in the home service space for over 15 years in Illinois, Kristin has experience on how a franchisee needs to adapt over time to changing circumstances. Having passed through multiple recessions, Kristin emphasizes the **need for business owners to have lines of credit and other financing mechanisms to meet payroll and other financial obligations during tough times.**

Kristin also offers franchise consulting services along with her colleagues at "Pillars of Franchising." Kristin gives advice to new franchisees in a manner that is honest, clear, and direct. She also supports existing franchisees in growing their business. It is worth noting that Kristin and her colleagues leverage Vetted Biz to bridge the information and data gaps while serving prospective and current franchisees.

Kristin believes that times have changed over the past 15 years and she has been fortunate to retain many of the same employees over the past decade. Hiring is always a challenge, but being part of a large, well-funded parent company (Neighborly) helps. Her focus had always been on developing a "family-run" brand versus a corporate brand. However, now Molly Maid is part of a large conglomerate and has become more corporate. She maintains that the pandemic had an impact on how long employees would stay with Molly Maid.

Currently, in Kristin's franchise, she has 25 employees, but could use another 10 people. Having the original vision and "beginning with the end in mind" have helped her succeed. A Molly Maid franchise also gave Kristin the ability to move around the country frequently because she did not necessarily need to be onsite with her business.

The first few years required hard work, and as the owner, Kristin set the core values for her team at the outset. Recognizing that different businesses have varying cultures, while maintaining high standards, helped Kristin achieve great success.

CHECKLIST

☐ Circle back to the financing consultant or your bank lender. Finalize the loan application and any other information you need to secure your financing.

☐ Make sure you have a business bank account set up.

☐ Make sure you get your Federal Tax Identification Number.

☐ Never sign an agreement where you commit money that you do not have yet without an exit ramp.

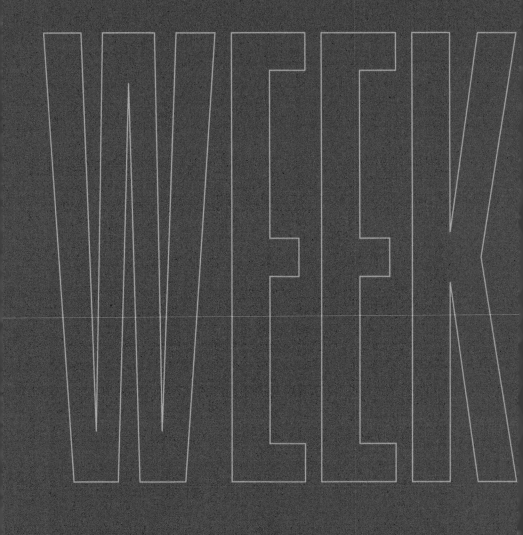

11

FRANCHISE ATTORNEY NEGOTIATES CONTRACT

"Let us never negotiate out of fear. But let us never fear to negotiate."

John F. Kennedy

"The most difficult thing in any negotiation almost, is making sure that you strip it of the emotion and deal with the facts."

Howard Baker

Negotiating your contract is absolutely necessary. If you do not negotiate your contract properly, you will end up with a version that might not work in your favor. In any event, always think "win-win."

Therefore, you should never sign your contract without negotiating. You should look at key terms like minimum royalty, and the ability to compete in the same industry if your business does not work out after two years. For instance, would you still be obligated for eight years of minimum royalties? All of these are issues you negotiate to assure alignment with your future business plans.

If the royalties are based on sales, you should only agree to pay a percentage of net sales, instead of gross sales. It would be beneficial to minimize any interest payable on past-due amounts.

There are also confidentiality considerations. While negotiating the franchise agreement it is crucial to limit overly burdensome or broad restrictions on the use and protection of the franchisor's confidential information, including any post-term obligations.

As a rule of thumb, you should prohibit the franchisor from unreasonably withholding, delaying, or conditioning consent to the assignment. Seek authority to transfer interests to or for the benefit of affiliates or family members for restructuring or estate planning purposes. Allow room in your agreement for the transferability of existing franchise agreements (rather than require a transferee to enter into a new agreement with the franchisor).

Your agreement should allow the franchisor to terminate the default only after the franchisee has had the opportunity and failed to cure the default. However, seek the right to terminate all or part of the franchise agreement for yourself. Try to get any non-compete or non-solicitation provisions modified in the event that the franchisor: breaches the agreement; fails to comply with applicable law; files for bankruptcy or becomes insolvent. If default triggers the right of the franchisor to purchase the business, seek fair market value for the franchised business and have it written into the contract.

The franchise agreement should not require the franchisee to agree to be governed, in any litigation relating to the franchise agreement or any other agreement between the parties, by the laws of any state other than the state in which the franchisee's business is located unless consent for the substitution is freely given and actually negotiated. No franchise agreement should limit any additional legal protections afforded to the franchisee's business under applicable state law.

Collective action is a fundamentally important method of resolving some disputes. Franchisees should be permitted to bring group or class actions on common issues, and franchisees should not be required to waive existing procedural or statutory rights to bring group or class actions on common issues.

There are issues that a good franchisor will be flexible with and other issues where they will be inflexible. Some of the inflexible items might include: royalties, brand development fees, and initial franchise fees. Some of the flexible items might include: the territory of your business, transfers in your family, and considerations for special circumstances.

Remember, if a franchisor is negotiating the initial franchise fee (besides military veteran discounts) or any of the other inflexible items, it might be possible that their business is desperate for franchisees. As such, you might want to do more research into the legal history of the business.

CHECKLIST

☐ In any event, always think "win-win."

☐ Negotiate the minimum royalty.

☐ Ability to compete in the same industry if your business does not work out.

☐ Limit overly burdensome or broad restrictions on the use and protection of the franchisor's confidential information, including any post-term obligations.

☐ Allow room in your agreement for the transferability of existing franchise agreements.

☐ Seek the right to terminate all or part of the franchise agreement for yourself.

12

SIGNING THE FRANCHISE AGREEMENT

"I do not think that there is any other quality so essential to success of any kind as the quality of perseverance. It overcomes almost everything, even nature."

John D. Rockefeller

Congratulations! You are well on your way to opening your franchise! This is the beginning of your journey to business success. All you need to do now is finalize the lease, get the business ready to operate, complete your training, and have a grand opening! (Remember, some franchisors will tell you at least how much they want you to spend on the opening.)

Now that your business is up and running, it is time to look forward to breaking even and starting to generate some profit for yourself. Start with a $5,000-a-month initial goal and slowly build up from there – the sky is the limit.

At this point, you might want to start reaching out to the top-performing franchisees that you can connect with. Talking with them will help you understand what you need to do to make your business better and how you can make it more efficient. Seek out mentors who can be helpful in your journey.

Lastly, but most importantly, do not let negativity drag you down. You have just started your business and there will be some people who will judge you unfairly very early. Do not listen to them and always stay persistent and positive. Businesses take some time to get off the ground but they can reap major financial rewards and provide fulfillment in your life ahead. Think of yourself as an endurance athlete with the finish line as your goal in mind!

CASE STUDY:

SCOTT GREENBERG

Author of the Wealthy Franchisee

Franchise Opened in 2005 and Sold in 2015

Previous Experience: Motivational Speaker

Franchise: Edible Arrangements

Scott Greenberg grew up as the son of a serial entrepreneur. Scott followed his father's journey closely, with all the success stories as well as the cautionary tales. Married to the daughter of a college professor who at the time had two jobs his entire life, Scott's wife looked at him as "crazy" for getting into a business he knew nothing about.

For years, Scott was a motivational speaker with a focus on resilience, peak performance, and leadership. Because it bothered him that many in his audience had more leadership experience than him, Scott decided to do something about it. He figured that an Edible Arrangements franchise would be a learning experience as well as a laboratory to try out different concepts. He found a connection between what was happening in the real world and his motivational speaking.

Scott learned through his mistakes and kept improving until he had the top Edible Arrangements location in California. Then he took over one of *the worst locations and turned it around. Ultimately, he received many invitations to speak before the franchise industry and has spoken with thousands of franchisees over the years. In so doing he has learned what makes a franchisee successful.*

While Scott had student leadership experience managing people, he had not done this in the business world. He decided to run his own business to get his "hands" dirty" and experience growing an enterprise firsthand.

In conducting his surveys of thousands of franchisees, he focused on performance, beliefs, and challenges. He found that the less successful franchisees tended to blame others instead of taking responsibility. While he did not talk directly to other franchises before opening his own, Scott would not recommend the approach he took.

But before signing on the line, he did speak with several franchisees, and visited an Edible Arrangements operation. The validation or due diligence process is critical for any entrepreneur seeking to become a franchisee. His questions covered such topics as cost, values, location, and culture. Scott was a franchisee in the Edible Arrangements organization for over 10 years, a solid run. Usually franchise agreements are 10 years, but could also be five or 20 years. Scott built his first store and then acquired a second store from a struggling franchisee. This was a case of FOMO, and Scott did not want to miss an opportunity. Moreover, Scott always admired the multi-unit operators at the Edible Arrangements conventions.

Scott never thought he would get rich through a franchise but rather saw this vehicle as a supplement to his motivational speaker income. His goal was not to be a multi-unit operator, but rather to be equipped to answer questions on stage. While most speakers are successful in their business before becoming speakers, Scott's angle as a speaker was overcoming adversity, having beaten cancer in his 20s. The emotional or human side of the franchise journey cannot be separated from the financial part. Having 10 years of material as a franchisee certainly gave him the material to go to a higher level as a motivational speaker.

While there is always competition, franchisee collaboration can be a win-win for everyone. Each franchisee should recognize that he is part of a larger brand. And if the brand does well, every franchisee is lifted up.

Franchisors build a brand as well as a culture, and they need to see when a prospective franchisee is not a good fit instead of just accepting every applicant. Franchisors need to have a vision and be selective so that all their franchisees have the same missions and objectives. In evaluating successful franchises, one should look at the sales matrix rather than franchise fees collected. The franchisor's management must have the broader vision than the business development experts. Building the right system with the right people should always be the goal.

Having other franchisees validating the brand and the system is important. While a number of franchisees will succeed with the right system, others will struggle and need to be lifted up by support from the franchisor through the franchise agreement. Essentially, Scott sees three groups in a given franchise: (1) top performers needing reinforcement; (2) middle performers needing a little push, encouragement, and perspective; and (3) struggling franchisees who resist the system and the help that is offered. Often the top performers can acquire the struggling ones.

On the interpersonal side, one of the top predictors of how well one will do running a franchise business is the level of support from their family. In a marriage, the other spouse needs to stand behind the entrepreneur to make the path easier to succeed. However, spousal support does not necessarily mean involvement. Other ingredients to succeed include being: "scrappy," having the ability to sell, analyzing the data, being logical, and having backup plans.

While maintaining two jobs (speaking and franchisee), Scott had to create leaders in his employees and delegate responsibility. He had to put systems in place, including regular communications, so the business could run when he was not physically present. Growing the business was as important as running the business. And everyone's time has a value.

Scott defines wealthy franchisees as making good money, but also in control of their time, with the ability to make choices and maintain a solid quality of life. In other words, wealth is not defined by money alone! You want to grow with your company and reach your potential without sacrificing your quality of life.

It is important to remember that the franchisee is the franchisor's customer. The consumer is the franchisee's customer. Measuring franchisee satisfaction can be found through "Franchise Business Review" or by speaking directly with current franchisees through validation calls and visits. One should look at profitability and culture (e.g., collaboration) and not just at franchise revenue.

To have a positive franchise culture there needs to be commitment, executed policies, a clear set of beliefs, and the same mission to support those beliefs. A similar, positive mindset is crucial. Other important aspects include having rituals to create bonding, transparency, and strong human interpersonal relationships.

CHECKLIST

☐ Start reaching out to the top-performing franchisees to learn how to make your business better and more efficient.

☐ Finalize the lease.

☐ Get the business ready to operate.

☐ Complete your training.

☐ Have a grand opening.

In closing, I will make an analogy with the ultimate physical endurance test, the marathon, having completed triathlons as well as the Boston Marathon with my father. Those runners enjoying the race the most are not doing it to beat a certain time.

They are running the marathon for the whole experience and oftentimes for a greater purpose such as raising money for a charity and/or in homage to a late family member. Their success will come at the end of the race and their life will be no different if they finish 10 minutes faster.

These 12 weeks have involved intensive training and preparation, sprints, and longer runs combined with introspection and investigation on how best to thrive as you move forward with your new business. You are now at the start line of the marathon, the most important race in your life, and you are ready to run a strong and solid race!

During a marathon, you should always keep your head high and not let minor distractions get in the way of your race. In business, you will follow the same approach. Stay positive and persistent. Work hard, but also have fun. Pace yourself and know when to alter your strategies. Begin with the end in mind. Always think success and that "failure is not an option."

In a marathon, there is no greater feeling than knowing you gave it your all and while so doing also helped others to make it through the grueling race. You keep your eyes focused ahead in the right direction and do not look back. You smile a lot and show gratitude to the volunteers at the aid stations providing water and food. You develop a camaraderie with fellow runners, all working toward a common goal of crossing that finish line.

Similarly, it will be important to rely on other franchisees as well as your franchisor when you become a business owner and entrepreneur. And you will be helping the other franchisees as well as the franchisor as you move forward. Like your fellow marathoners, you are all in this together.

The best way to thrive in a marathon is to prepare properly both mentally and physically. There is no greater feeling in one day of physical tenacity than crossing that finish line in the marathon.

We know that you will feel the same as you see success in your future business. We hope that our 12-week program will give you all the necessary tools to become an entrepreneur and run a strong race until you get to the finish line!

ACKNOWLE

DGMENTS

Writing and publishing this book has truly been a team effort. I want to thank my father, Joe, for his support in structuring the book and especially with the case studies. My colleagues from Vetted Biz, Marina Longo and Abi Moreno, supported with the formatting, copy, and graphics. Also, Parth Parth, who is a student at my alma mater, Colby College, has written hundreds of franchise analyses of which many were fundamental for this book. Dave Aretha did a great job proofreading the book on a tight schedule.

The book would not have been possible without the hundreds of franchisees and franchisors I interviewed from 2015 to 2022. Their insights have been crucial to the content of this book.

My father taught me to be curious about other people, cultures, and opportunities. That has directly led to my career in information services and more and more into content creation.

My brother Jack has been my business partner for 7+ years. Jack has pushed me to be the best manager/ brother/ person I possibly can be. I would not be where I am professionally without the sounding board and complementary skill set that Jack provides. His feedback on the book was on point too, as expected.

My brother Mark helped us grow our business presence in Mexico and Latin America. I've learned a tremendous amount about how to best bridge cultures from Mark's experience as an expat in Mexico City and his work with our clients.

My mother, Rosemary, taught me the importance of mastering the art of conversation. Her deceased sister, Kate Walsh O'Beirne, editor and columnist, was an incredible interviewer on television, and I'm sure she had honed her skills while growing up in the same household as my mother and her sisters.

My mother's strong Catholic faith has inspired me to help people as much as possible and stay committed to our Christian values. Prospective franchisees and business owners deserve to know what operating a business is truly like and should not be taken advantage of.

My wife, Emilie, has continued to support my career and all the effort required to publishing this book. Even if that meant missing dinners and late nights, she understood that this is part of my vocation and encouraged me to see my work through.

And last but not least, my toddler daughter, Olivia. You have taught me "there's no time like the present," whether you are working or having fun.

Introduction

- www.vettedbiz.com

- https://www.sba.gov/business-guide/plan-your-business/buy-existing-business-or-franchise/sba-franchise-directory

Week 1

- https://www.vettedbiz.com/wendys-franchise/

Week 2

- https://www.sba.gov/partners/lenders/7a-loan-program/terms-conditions-eligibility

- https://www.steaknshakefranchise.com/

- https://www.chick-fil-a.com/

Week 3

- https://www.aafd.org/

- https://www.wework.com/

- https://www.regus.com/en-us

Week 4

- https://www.marketdataenterprises.com/autism-treatment-programs-market-bigger-than-thought-4-billionb/

- https://franchise.teriyakimadness.com/

- https://www.smoothiekingfranchise.com/

- https://go.ownamericanfreight.com/

- American Freight Email Sent From Franchise Times (2022-07-21)

- Top Global Franchises: https://www.entrepreneur.com/franchises/9roundfitness/334179

2021 & 2022 Franchise Disclosure Documents (FDD) for the following brands:

- Teriyaki Madness: https://www.vettedbiz.com/wp-content/uploads/wpallimport/files/teriyaki-madness-2022-fdd.pdf

- Domino's: https://www.vettedbiz.com/wp-content/uploads/wpallimport/files/dominos-2022-fdd.pdf

- Papa John's: https://www.vettedbiz.com/wp-content/uploads/wpallimport/files/papa-johns-2022-fdd.pdf

- Marco's Pizza: https://www.vettedbiz.com/wp-content/uploads/wpallimport/files/marcos-pizza-2022-fdd.pdf

- Blaze Pizza: https://www.vettedbiz.com/wp-content/uploads/wpallimport/files/blaze-pizza-2022-fdd.pdf

- Little Caesars: https://www.vettedbiz.com/wp-content/uploads/wpallimport/files/little-caesars-2022-fdd.pdf

- Pizza Hut Traditional: https://www.vettedbiz.com/wp-content/uploads/wpallimport/files/pizza-hut-traditional-2022-fdd.pdf

- Home Instead: https://www.vettedbiz.com/wp-content/uploads/wpallimport/files/home-instead-2022-fdd.pdf

- Synergy HomeCare: https://www.vettedbiz.com/wp-content/uploads/wpallimport/files/synergy-homecare-2022-fdd.pdf

- BrighStar Care: https://www.vettedbiz.com/wp-content/uploads/wpallimport/files/brightstar-care-2022-fdd.pdf

- Right at Home: https://www.vettedbiz.com/wp-content/uploads/wpallimport/files/right-at-home-2022-fdd.pdf

- Senior Helpers: https://www.vettedbiz.com/senior-helpers-franchise/

- Touching Hearts at Home: https://www.vettedbiz.com/wp-content/uploads/wpallimport/files/touching-hearts-2021-fdd.pdf

- Visiting Angels: https://www.vettedbiz.com/wp-content/uploads/wpallimport/files/visiting-angels-living-assistance-services-2022-fdd.pdf

- FirstLight HomeCare: https://www.vettedbiz.com/wp-content/uploads/wpallimport/files/firstlight-home-care-2022-fdd.pdf

- Interim HealthCare: https://www.vettedbiz.com/wp-content/uploads/wpallimport/files/interim-healthcare-2022-fdd.pdf

- Assisting Hands HomeCare: https://www.vettedbiz.com/wp-content/uploads/wpallimport/files/assisting-hands-home-care-2022-fdd.pdf

- https://www.vettedbiz.com/40-worst-franchises-by-sba-loan/

- https://www.vettedbiz.com/top-20-franchises/

- https://www.vettedbiz.com/20-franchise-investments-avoid/

Week 5

- Franchise Flippers: https://franchiseflippers.com/

- Franchise ReSales: https://www.franchiseresales.com/

- Biz Buy Sell: https://www.bizbuysell.com/

- https://www.unhappyfranchisee.com/category/franchisor/snap-on/
  https://www.unhappyfranchisee.com/category/franchisor/dickeys-barbecue-pit-franchise-franchisor/

- Burgerim (Vehicle): https://www.ftc.gov/news-events/news/press-releases/2022/02/ftc-sues-burger-franchise-company-targets-veterans-others-false-promises-misleading-documents

- Nestle USA: https://www.law360.com/articles/849856/nestle-usa-sues-franchisee-for-going-too-far-with-its-ip

- Snap-on: https://www.unhappyfranchisee.com/category/franchisor/snap-on/HYPERLINK "https://www.unhappyfranchisee.com/category/franchisor/snap-on/"

- Dickey's BBQ: https://www.unhappyfranchisee.com/category/franchisor/dickeys-barbecue-pit-franchise-franchisor/

- https://www.ftc.gov/news-events/news/press-releases/2022/02/ftc-sues-burger-franchise-company-targets-veterans-others-false-promises-misleading-documents

- https://casetext.com/case/lockhart-v-home-grown-industries-of-georgia

- https://www.youtube.com/watch?v=WjtuY18G-iE

- https://www.law360.com/cases/57f8134e24df9e2511000006/articles

- Planet Beach 2021 FDD: https://www.vettedbiz.com/wp-content/uploads/wpallimport/files/planet-beach-2021-fdd.pdf

- F45 Training 2022 FDD: https://www.vettedbiz.com/wp-content/uploads/wpallimport/files/f45-training-2022-fdd.pdf

- Anytime Fitness 2022 FDD: https://www.vettedbiz.com/wp-content/uploads/wpallimport/files/anytime-fitness-2022-fdd.pdf

- Crumbl 2022 FDD: https://www.vettedbiz.com/wp-content/uploads/wpallimport/files/crumbl-2022-fdd.pdf

- https://www.vettedbiz.com/franchisee-sued-for-royalty-payments/

Week 11

- https://www.aafd.org/fairness-initiatives/fair-franchising-standards/

Made in the USA
Las Vegas, NV
03 September 2024

94730815R00077